Delicious High-Protein Low-Calorie Snacks 100 Inspiring Pictures

Quick & Original Recipes with Best Ideas for Every Snack Time!

By Oliver Brentwood

Copyright © 2023 by Oliver Brentwood

All rights reserved. This book, "**Delicious High-Protein Low-Calorie Snacks 100 Inspiring Pictures** " including its subtitle "**Quick & Original Recipes with Best Ideas for Every Snack Time!** "or any portion of its contents may not be reproduced, copied, modified, or adapted, without the prior written consent of the author, unless otherwise indicated for stand-alone materials.

This publication is designed to provide accurate and authoritative information in regard to the subject matter covered. It is provided with the understanding that the author and the publisher are not engaged in rendering medical, health, psychological, or any other kind of personal professional services. If the reader requires personal medical, health, or other assistance or advice, a competent professional should be consulted.

The author and the publisher specifically disclaim all responsibility for any liability, loss, or risk, personal or otherwise, which is incurred as a consequence, directly or indirectly, of the use and application of any of the contents of this book.

No part of this publication may be reproduced, stored in a retrieval system, or transmitted in any form or by any means, electronic, mechanical, photocopying, recording, scanning, or otherwise, except as permitted under Section 107 or 108 of the 1976 United States Copyright Act, without the prior written permission of the author.

Introduction

Delicious High-Protein Low-Calorie Snacks 100 Inspiring Pictures

Have you ever found yourself rummaging through the pantry, desperately seeking a snack that's not just tasty but also nutritious? It's a common problem: craving something delicious yet won't derail our health goals.

Dive into a treasure trove of mouthwatering snacks that perfectly balance indulgence and nutrition. Oliver Brentwood has curated a selection of 100 snack ideas, each high in protein and low in calories. But these aren't just ordinary snacks; they're culinary masterpieces made simple for everyday enjoyment. Whether you're a seasoned chef or a kitchen novice, these recipes, backed by inspiring photos, will reignite your love for snacking.

Imagine having a list of snacks that will satiate your hunger and fuel your body with the protein it needs. From savory bites to sweet treats, each recipe has been crafted to ensure you don't compromise on taste while keeping those extra calories at bay. The vibrant photos accompanying each recipe are more than just eye candy—they're your roadmap, beckoning you to recreate these edible artworks in your kitchen.

So, ready to elevate your snack game? Open the pages of this book, be it Kindle or Paperback, and embark on a delightful journey that promises an array of flavors, aromas, and textures. Say goodbye to the mundane and embrace snack times that are as wholesome as delectable. Let **"Delicious High-Protein, Low-Calorie Snacks 100 Inspiring Pictures "** be your trusty guide to creating quick, original, and best snack ideas for every craving and occasion.

Indulge healthfully, snack creatively, and enjoy each bite with Oliver Brentwood's gourmet touch. Happy snacking!

by Oliver Brentwood

Table of Contents

Chapter 01: Morning Fuel-Up 8
Recipe 01: Banana Pancake Stack with Strawberry and Hazelnut Cream ...8

Recipe 02: Breakfast Muffins Morning Glory 10

Recipe 03: Oatmeal with Banana Nuts and Berries 12

Recipe 04: Quinoa Porridge with Apples and Cinnamon 14

Recipe 05: Dark Almond Chocolate Bars 16

Recipe 06: Energy Protein Balls 18

Recipe 07: Milk Pudding with Caramel Syrup 20

Recipe 08: Dates Syrup 22

Recipe 09: Delicious Egg Muffins with Pepper 24

Recipe 10: Grain Toast Topped with Almond Butter 26

Chapter 02: Brunch Bites 28
Recipe 11: Turkey Burger with Sweet Potato 28

Recipe 12: Sweet Mix Fruits Topping on Milk Tofu 30

Recipe 13: Fried Eggs in Tomato Sauce 32

Recipe 14: Eggs Benedict 34

Recipe 15: Berry Bread Pudding with Mulberries 36

Recipe 16: Bliss Avocado-Baked Egg on Toast 38

Recipe 17: Mini Cheese Burger Buns 40

Recipe 18: Frittata with Grilled Summer Vegetables Baked 42

Recipe 19: Cheesecake for Agar-Agar with Cherries and Almonds 44

Recipe 20: Healthy Match Bliss Energy Balls with Dates Hemp and Nuts 46

Chapter 03: Lunch Lifters 48
Recipe 21: Power Salad with Black Beans Avocado and Cooked White Rice 48

Recipe 22: Teriyaki Tofu Rice Bowl 50

Recipe 23: Quinoa with Vegetables 52

Recipe 24: Delicious Salad with Anchovies and Battered Cheese 54

Recipe 25: Vegan Pasta with Carrots Celeri and Fresh Pesto Sauce 56

- Recipe 26: Golden Lentil Spinach Soup 58
- Recipe 27: Healthy Asian Chicken Lettuce Wrap with Carrots 60
- Recipe 28: Roast Beef Rocket and Horseradish Sandwich 62
- Recipe 29: Grilled Chicken Salad 64
- Recipe 30: Delicious Veggie Bowl with Cucumber 66

Chapter 04: Afternoon Energizers 68
- Recipe 31: Energy Candy Balls Made of Chickpeas Dates and Pistachios 68
- Recipe 32: Chocolate Vegan Brownie Cake 70
- Recipe 33: Raw Organic Homemade Trail Mix with Nuts and Fruits 72
- Recipe 34: Nachos with Green Guacamole 74
- Recipe 35: Delicious Roasted Almonds and Large Pieces 76
- Recipe 36: Peanut Butter and Oatmeal Energy Balls 78
- Recipe 37: Payes With Cinnamon 80
- Recipe 38: Brown Creamy Cocktail Glass 82
- Recipe 39: Blueberry Squares with Crunchy Topping 84
- Recipe 40: Chocolate Pomegranate Banana Peanut Butter Shake 86

Chapter 05: Dinner Delights 88
- Recipe 41: Minced Beef Bolognese Sauce Topped 88
- Recipe 42: Kale Quinoa Salad with a Grilled Steak 90
- Recipe 43: Vegetarian Homemade Pie Quiche with Tomatoes 92
- Recipe 44: Chicken Breasts Cooked on a Summer BBQ 94
- Recipe 45: Vegan Strudel with Lentils 96
- Recipe 46: Fish and Tamarind-Based Soup 98
- Recipe 47: Baked Salmon Served with Chips 100
- Recipe 48: Spaghetti Squash with Marinara and Meatballs 102
- Recipe 49: Beef Stew Cooked with Pomegranate and Herbs 104
- Recipe 50: Eggplant Chickpeas Peas Vegetarian Vegan Curry 106

Chapter 06: Midnight Munchies 108
- Recipe 51: Vegan Chocolate Truffles Balls 108

Recipe 52: Peanut Butter Sandwich Vegetarian Food 110

Recipe 53: Grilled Salmon Trout Fish with Spices Lemon.......................112

Recipe 54: Fresh Popcorn with Chili Pepper..114

Recipe 55: Muesli Bar Partially Covered with Dry Fruits and One Bit 116

Recipe 56: Slice of Vegan Cheesecake Made with Plant Protein Powder 118

Recipe 57: Freshly Baked Blueberry Muffins 120

Recipe 58: Cake with Chocolate and Sea Salt..122

Recipe 59: A Nutty Milk Chocolate Coated Brownies 124

Recipe 60: Pancakes..126

Chapter 07: Seafood Specials 128

Recipe 61: Seared Portuguese Scallops in a White Wine Lemon Garlic Sauce
....128

Recipe 62: Cilantro-Lime Grilled Tuna with Avocado Cucumber Salsa ..130

Recipe 63: A Delicious Salmon Burger with Lettuce 132

Recipe 64: Zucchini Salad with Prawns Flatley on a Marble Countertop 134

Recipe 65: Steamed Cod with Olive Tapenade 136

Recipe 66: Pumpkin Soup with Quinoa and Spinach 138

Recipe 67: Beautiful Still Life of Boiled Corn...140

Recipe 68: Mahi Fish Sandwich with Salsa and Lettuce 142

Recipe 69: Japanese Deep-Fried Crispy Tempura Prawn 144

Recipe 70: Roasted Fish with Almond and Salad.......................................146

Chapter 08: Sip & Savor Smoothies..148

Recipe 71: Red and Pink Smoothies 148

Recipe 72: Christmas Sugar Cookie White Russian Cocktail....................150

Recipe 73: Energy Berry Bliss Balls of Desiccated Coconut Mixed.........152

Recipe 74: Hot Mocha Coffee 154

Recipe 75: Trendy Comfort Snack Crispy Roasted Crushed Potatoes 156

Recipe 76: Making Juice with Mango Fruit 158

Recipe 77: Beautifully Decorated Muffins...160

Recipe 78: Grilled Chicken with Rice 162

Recipe 79: Baked Chicken with Fruits and Greens 164
Recipe 80: Fresh Baked Chocolate Rolls 166

Chapter 09: Salad Satisfiers 168

Recipe 81: Grilled Chicken Breast in Different Variation 168
Recipe 82: Delicious Mediterranean Green Shakshuka Fried with Eggs . 170
Recipe 83: Soft Focus Raw Beef Spicy Minced Meat Salad 172
Recipe 84: Peppers Grill Baked Vegetable Pepper Grilled 174
Recipe 85: Tuscan Bean and Tuna Salad with Tomatoes 176
Recipe 86: Healthy Tempeh Tacos Dripping 178
Recipe 87: Chickpea Soup Moroccan Traditional Dish 180
Recipe 88: Avocado Greek Yogurt Sauce 182
Recipe 89: Spicy Southwestern Chicken Salad 184
Recipe 90: Sliced Steak of Tuna in Sesame and a Salad 186

Chapter 10: Dessert Decadence 188

Recipe 92: Lemon Cheesecake 190
Recipe 93: Mousse Cake Made of Chocolate 192
Recipe 94: Asty Chocolate Wedding Cake Decorated with Berries 194
Recipe 95: Pecan Pie Brownie Bars Drizzled with Caramel Sauce 196
Recipe 96: Blueberry Crumble with a Scoop of Vanilla Ice Cream 198
Recipe 97: Dark Raw Chocolate with Hazelnut 200
Recipe 98: Strawberry Shortcake Ice Cream Bars with Cake Crumbles ... 202
Recipe 99: Delicious Freshly Baked Cinnamon Rolls 204
Recipe 100: Matcha Green Tea Ice Cream 206

Conclusion 208

Chapter 01: Morning Fuel-Up

Recipe 01: Banana Pancake Stack with Strawberry and Hazelnut Cream

Kickstart your morning with a delightful Banana Pancake Stack drizzled with strawberry and hazelnut cream. This breakfast dish is delicious and packed with essential nutrients to fuel your day.

Servings: 4

Prepping Time: 15 minutes

Cook Time: 20 minutes

Difficulty: Medium

Ingredients:

- ✓ 2 ripe bananas, mashed & 1 cup all-purpose flour
- ✓ 1 teaspoon baking powder & 1/4 teaspoon salt
- ✓ 1 cup milk & 2 large eggs

- ✓ 1/2 cup strawberry puree
- ✓ 1/2 cup hazelnut cream
- ✓ 1 tablespoon unsalted butter for cooking
- ✓ Fresh strawberries, for garnish
- ✓ Chopped hazelnuts for garnish

Step-by-Step Preparation:

1. Combine mashed bananas, flour, baking powder, and salt in a mixing bowl.
2. In a separate bowl, whisk together milk and eggs. Gradually add this to the banana mixture.
3. Heat a skillet over medium heat and melt a bit of butter.
4. Pour 1/4 cup of batter for each pancake. Cook until bubbles form on the surface, then flip and cook until golden.
5. Stack pancakes on a plate and drizzle with strawberry puree and hazelnut cream.
6. Garnish with fresh strawberries and chopped hazelnuts. Serve warm.

Nutritional Facts: (Per serving)

- ➢ Calories: 320
- ➢ Protein: 9g
- ➢ Carbohydrates: 42g
- ➢ Dietary Fiber: 3g
- ➢ Sugars: 12g
- ➢ Fat: 14g
- ➢ Saturated Fat: 5g
- ➢ Cholesterol: 95mg
- ➢ Sodium: 250mg

Indulging in a Banana Pancake Stack with Strawberry and Hazelnut Cream is the perfect way to infuse energy and taste into your morning routine. Satisfy your sweet cravings and fuel your body with this delightful dish to conquer the day ahead.

Recipe 02: Breakfast Muffins Morning Glory

Wake up to the aroma of freshly baked Breakfast Muffins Morning Glory, an ideal blend of nutrition and taste. These muffins guarantee an energetic start to any day.

Servings: 12

Prepping Time: 20 minutes

Cook Time: 25 minutes

Difficulty: Easy

Ingredients:

- 2 cups whole wheat flour
- 1 teaspoon baking soda
- 1/4 teaspoon salt
- 1/2 cup honey or maple syrup
- 1/4 cup melted coconut oil
- 2 large eggs

- ✓ 1 cup grated carrot
- ✓ 1/2 cup grated apple
- ✓ 1/4 cup raisins
- ✓ 1/4 cup chopped walnuts
- ✓ 1 teaspoon vanilla extract
- ✓ 1/2 cup plain yogurt or buttermilk

Step-by-Step Preparation:

1. Preheat the oven to 375°F (190°C) and line a muffin tin with liners.
2. In a large bowl, combine flour, baking soda, and salt.
3. Mix honey, coconut oil, eggs, and vanilla extract in another bowl.
4. Gradually mix the wet ingredients into the dry ones.
5. Fold in carrot, apple, raisins, and walnuts.
6. Stir in the yogurt until just combined.
7. Distribute the batter evenly among the muffin cups.
8. Bake for 22-25 minutes, or until a toothpick inserted comes out clean. Cool before serving.

Nutritional Facts: (Per serving)

- ➢ Calories: 185
- ➢ Protein: 4g
- ➢ Carbohydrates: 28g
- ➢ Dietary Fiber: 3g
- ➢ Sugars: 15g
- ➢ Fat: 7g
- ➢ Saturated Fat: 4g
- ➢ Cholesterol: 31mg
- ➢ Sodium: 150mg

The Breakfast Muffins Morning Glory seamlessly marry health and flavor, making them a preferred choice for those bustling mornings. These muffins are the perfect morning companion to kick off a productive day.

Recipe 03: Oatmeal with Banana Nuts and Berries

Begin your morning with a hearty bowl of Oatmeal with Banana Nuts and Berries. This nutritious and satisfying dish combines the warmth of oats with the natural sweetness of fruits, offering a vibrant start to your day.

Servings: 4

Prepping Time: 5 minutes

Cook Time: 10 minutes

Difficulty: Easy

Ingredients:

- ✓ 2 cups rolled oats
- ✓ 4 cups milk or water
- ✓ 2 ripe bananas, sliced
- ✓ 1/4 cup mixed nuts (walnuts, almonds, pecans), chopped
- ✓ 1/2 cup mixed berries (blueberries, raspberries, strawberries)

- ✓ 1 tablespoon honey or maple syrup (optional)
- ✓ 1/4 teaspoon vanilla extract
- ✓ Pinch of salt

Step-by-Step Preparation:

1. In a pot, bring milk or water to a boil.
2. Add oats, salt, and vanilla extract. Reduce heat and simmer, stirring occasionally.
3. Cook until the oats have absorbed the liquid and are tender about 5-7 minutes.
4. Remove from heat and stir in the sliced bananas and nuts.
5. Divide the oatmeal into bowls. Top with mixed berries and drizzle with honey or maple syrup, if desired.

Nutritional Facts: (Per serving)

- ➢ Calories: 290
- ➢ Protein: 9g
- ➢ Carbohydrates: 48g
- ➢ Dietary Fiber: 7g
- ➢ Sugars: 15g
- ➢ Fat: 8g
- ➢ Saturated Fat: 1.5g
- ➢ Cholesterol: 5mg
- ➢ Sodium: 80mg

Oatmeal with Banana Nuts and Berries is not just a breakfast dish; it's an experience. Each spoonful is a fusion of textures and flavors, promising wholesome nutrition. It's a meal that sets the tone for a day full of potential and energy.

Recipe 04: Quinoa Porridge with Apples and Cinnamon

Elevate your breakfast routine with Quinoa Porridge with Apples and Cinnamon. A modern twist on traditional porridge, this dish melds the nuttiness of quinoa with sweet apples, creating an energizing start to your day.

Servings: 4

Prepping Time: 10 minutes

Cook Time: 20 minutes

Difficulty: Easy

Ingredients:

- ✓ 1 cup quinoa, rinsed and drained
- ✓ 2 cups milk (dairy or plant-based)
- ✓ 2 medium apples, diced
- ✓ 2 teaspoons ground cinnamon

- ✓ 1 tablespoon honey or maple syrup
- ✓ 1/4 cup chopped walnuts or almonds (optional)
- ✓ Pinch of salt
- ✓ Fresh apple slices and extra cinnamon for garnish

Step-by-Step Preparation:

1. Combine quinoa, milk, diced apples, and salt in a saucepan. Bring to a boil.
2. Reduce heat to low, cover, and let simmer for 15-20 minutes or until quinoa is tender and the milk is mostly absorbed.
3. Stir in cinnamon and honey or maple syrup.
4. Serve in bowls, garnished with fresh apple slices, a sprinkle of cinnamon, and nuts if desired.

Nutritional Facts: (Per serving)

- ➢ Calories: 220
- ➢ Protein: 7g
- ➢ Carbohydrates: 40g
- ➢ Dietary Fiber: 5g
- ➢ Sugars: 14g
- ➢ Fat: 4g
- ➢ Saturated Fat: 1g
- ➢ Cholesterol: 5mg
- ➢ Sodium: 60mg

Quinoa Porridge with Apples and Cinnamon is the ultimate fusion of health and comfort. A dish that warms the soul and ensures sustained energy for the day, it's a delightful departure from the everyday breakfast, wrapping you in a comforting embrace.

Recipe 05: Dark Almond Chocolate Bars

Indulge your mornings with the decadent allure of Dark Almond Chocolate Bars. These bars offer a luxurious yet energizing way to start your day.

Servings: 8

Prepping Time: 15 minutes

Cook Time: 2 hours (chilling)

Difficulty: Easy

Ingredients:

- 200g high-quality dark chocolate (70% cocoa or above)
- 1 cup roasted almonds, coarsely chopped
- 1 tablespoon coconut oil
- 1/4 teaspoon sea salt
- 2 tablespoons honey or maple syrup (optional)

Step-by-Step Preparation:

1. Mix dark chocolate and coconut oil using a double boiler or microwave.
2. Once melted, stir in honey or maple syrup if a sweeter taste is desired.
3. Mix in the roasted almonds, ensuring they are well-coated with the chocolate.
4. Spread the mixture evenly on a parchment-lined tray or silicone mold.
5. Sprinkle with sea salt.
6. Chill in the refrigerator for at least 2 hours or until set.
7. Once set, break or cut into bars.

Nutritional Facts: (Per serving)

- Calories: 240
- Protein: 5g
- Carbohydrates: 18g
- Dietary Fiber: 4g
- Sugars: 10g
- Fat: 18g
- Saturated Fat: 8g
- Cholesterol: 0mg
- Sodium: 80mg

Dark Almond Chocolate Bars redefine morning indulgence. These bars aren't just a treat but also a nourishing fuel that awakens the senses. Their deep cocoa flavors, punctuated by crunchy almonds, ensure a morning as memorable as the taste lingering on your palate.

Recipe 06: Energy Protein Balls

Jumpstart your mornings with Energy Protein Balls packed with healthful ingredients. These bite-sized morsels are a symphony of nutrition and taste, ensuring your day begins energetically.

Servings: 15 balls

Prepping Time: 20 minutes

Cook Time: No cook (chilling time: 30 minutes)

Difficulty: Easy

Ingredients:

- 1 cup rolled oats
- 1/2 cup natural peanut butter or almond butter
- 1/4 cup honey or maple syrup
- 1/2 cup ground flaxseed
- 1/2 cup chocolate chips or cacao nibs
- 2 tablespoons chia seeds

- ✓ 1 teaspoon vanilla extract
- ✓ A pinch of salt

Step-by-Step Preparation:

1. Combine rolled oats, peanut butter, honey, ground flaxseed, and chia seeds in a large mixing bowl.
2. Stir in chocolate chips, vanilla extract, and a pinch of salt until well combined.
3. Shape the mixture into small balls using your hands.
4. Place the protein balls on a parchment-lined tray or plate.
5. Refrigerate for at least 30 minutes to firm up before serving.

Nutritional Facts: (Per serving)

- ➢ Calories: 130
- ➢ Protein: 4g
- ➢ Carbohydrates: 15g
- ➢ Dietary Fiber: 3g
- ➢ Sugars: 8g
- ➢ Fat: 7g
- ➢ Saturated Fat: 1.5g
- ➢ Cholesterol: 0mg
- ➢ Sodium: 40mg

Every bite of the Energy Protein Balls is an invitation to wellness and vitality. Easy to make and even easier to enjoy, these power-packed spheres are your perfect morning allies. Whether you're rushing out or savoring a slow start, they ensure every dawn is filled with nourishing energy.

Recipe 07: Milk Pudding with Caramel Syrup

Indulge in the velvety smoothness of Milk Pudding with Caramel Syrup, a delightful morning treat. The subtle sweetness of the pudding harmoniously blends with the rich caramel, offering a luscious start to the day.

Servings: 4

Prepping Time: 15 minutes

Cook Time: 2 hours (including setting time)

Difficulty: Moderate

Ingredients:

- ✓ 2 cups whole milk
- ✓ 1/4 cup granulated sugar (for pudding)
- ✓ 1/4 cup granulated sugar (for caramel)
- ✓ 2 tablespoons cornstarch & 1/4 teaspoon vanilla extract
- ✓ A pinch of salt & 1/4 cup water

Step-by-Step Preparation:

1. Heat 1/4 cup sugar and water on medium heat in a saucepan, swirling occasionally, until amber caramel forms. Pour into individual ramekins, tilting to coat the base.
2. In another saucepan, warm the milk, but don't let it boil.
3. Whisk together 1/4 cup sugar, cornstarch, and salt in a bowl.
4. Gradually whisk the warm milk and transfer the mixture to the saucepan.
5. Cook over medium heat, stirring continuously, until the mixture thickens.
6. Remove from heat, stir in vanilla, and pour the mixture into the caramel-coated ramekins.
7. Chill in the refrigerator for at least 2 hours or until set.

Nutritional Facts: (Per serving)

- Calories: 170
- Protein: 4g
- Carbohydrates: 32g
- Dietary Fiber: 0g
- Sugars: 28g
- Fat: 3.5g
- Saturated Fat: 2g
- Cholesterol: 15mg
- Sodium: 80mg

Milk Pudding with Caramel Syrup adds luxury to your morning rituals. A balance between creamy softness and decadent sweetness, this dish ensures your day commences with a hint of luxury and abundant delight. Embrace this breakfast delicacy and savor every sumptuous spoonful.

Recipe 08: Dates Syrup

Dates Syrup Overhead View is a delightful morning elixir, enhancing any breakfast dish with its rich, natural sweetness. This syrup provides an energy boost with a touch of nature's goodness.

Servings: 10

Prepping Time: 10 minutes

Cook Time: 25 minutes

Difficulty: Easy

Ingredients:

- 1 cup pitted dates
- 1 1/2 cups water
- 1/2 teaspoon lemon juice
- A pinch of salt

Step-by-Step Preparation:

1. In a saucepan, combine pitted dates and water. Let it soak for about 1 hour.
2. Bring the mixture to a simmer over medium heat.
3. Cook until dates are very soft, and the mixture thickens, about 20 minutes.
4. Remove from heat and blend the mixture using a blender until smooth.
5. Stir in lemon juice and a pinch of salt.
6. Strain the syrup using a fine-mesh sieve and let it cool.

Nutritional Facts: (Per serving)

- Calories: 50
- Protein: 0.5g
- Carbohydrates: 13g
- Dietary Fiber: 1.5g
- Sugars: 11g
- Fat: 0g
- Saturated Fat: 0g
- Cholesterol: 0mg
- Sodium: 10mg

Dates Syrup Overhead View is more than a sweetener; it's an experience. Drizzle over your pancakes, oatmeal, or yogurt, and let its caramel-like notes elevate your morning dishes. Celebrate pure ingredients' simplicity while infusing your breakfast with a taste reminiscent of nature's finest.

Recipe 09: Delicious Egg Muffins with Pepper

Embark on a morning culinary journey with Delicious Egg Muffins with Pepper. These savory bites, enriched with the vibrant taste of peppers, provide a protein-packed start, ensuring your mornings are as flavorful as they are energized.

Servings: 6

Prepping Time: 10 minutes

Cook Time: 20 minutes

Difficulty: Easy

Ingredients:

- 6 large eggs
- 1/2 cup bell peppers (red, green, or yellow), diced
- 1/4 cup onions, finely chopped
- 1/4 cup shredded cheese (optional)
- Salt and pepper to taste

- ✓ 2 tablespoons milk
- ✓ Fresh parsley or chives for garnish

Step-by-Step Preparation:

1. Preheat oven to 375°F (190°C) and lightly grease a muffin tin.
2. Whisk together eggs, milk, salt, and pepper in a mixing bowl until well combined.
3. Stir in the diced bell peppers, onions, and cheese.
4. Pour the egg mixture into the muffin tins, filling each about 3/4 full.
5. Bake for 20 minutes or until the centers are set.
6. Allow cooling slightly before serving. Garnish with fresh parsley or chives.

Nutritional Facts: (Per serving)

- ➤ Calories: 90
- ➤ Protein: 7g
- ➤ Carbohydrates: 2g
- ➤ Dietary Fiber: 0.5g
- ➤ Sugars: 1g
- ➤ Fat: 6g
- ➤ Saturated Fat: 2g
- ➤ Cholesterol: 185mg
- ➤ Sodium: 80mg

Delicious Egg Muffins with Pepper are the epitome of morning convenience and delight. Their rich taste, combined with the crunchy freshness of bell peppers, ensures each bite is an explosion of flavor. Perfect for on-the-go or a leisurely breakfast at home, these muffins bring nutrition and zest.

Recipe 10: Grain Toast Topped with Almond Butter

Elevate your morning routine with the wholesome delight of Grain Toast Topped with Almond Butter. A symphony of crunch and creamy, this dish is delicious and a nutritional powerhouse to kickstart your day.

Servings: 2

Prepping Time: 5 minutes

Cook Time: 2 minutes

Difficulty: Easy

Ingredients:

- ✓ 2 slices of whole-grain bread
- ✓ 4 tablespoons almond butter
- ✓ A sprinkle of chia seeds (optional)
- ✓ A drizzle of honey or maple syrup (optional)
- ✓ A pinch of sea salt

Step-by-Step Preparation:

1. Toast the whole grain bread slices until they're golden brown and crispy.
2. Generously spread almond butter over each toast slice.
3. If desired, sprinkle with chia seeds and drizzle with honey or maple syrup for added sweetness.
4. Finish with a pinch of sea salt for a flavor boost.

Nutritional Facts: (Per serving)

- Calories: 220
- Protein: 7g
- Carbohydrates: 24g
- Dietary Fiber: 4g
- Sugars: 4g (excluding added sweeteners)
- Fat: 12g
- Saturated Fat: 1g
- Cholesterol: 0mg
- Sodium: 150mg

Grain Toast Topped with Almond Butter is the morning dish where simplicity meets nutrition. Every bite offers a delightful contrast of textures, from the hearty toast to the velvety almond spread. Whether in a rush or taking things slow, this toast promises a nourishing start filled with energy and flavor.

Chapter 02: Brunch Bites

Recipe 11: Turkey Burger with Sweet Potato

It introduces the Turkey Burger with Sweet Potato Waffle Fries, a brunch sensation that marries lean protein with a sweet and crispy side. This contemporary twist on the classic burger and fries combo promises a flavorful escape, perfect for midday indulgence.

Servings: 4

Prepping Time: 20 minutes

Cook Time: 30 minutes

Difficulty: Moderate

Ingredients:

- ✓ 1 lb. ground turkey & 1/2 cup breadcrumbs
- ✓ 1 large egg & 1 teaspoon garlic powder & 1 teaspoon onion powder
- ✓ Salt and pepper to taste & 4 burger buns

- ✓ Lettuce, tomatoes, and condiments of choice
- ✓ 2 large sweet potatoes, cut into waffle fries & 2 tablespoons olive oil
- ✓ 1/2 teaspoon smoked paprika

Step-by-Step Preparation:

1. Preheat oven to 425°F (220°C).
2. Combine ground turkey, breadcrumbs, egg, garlic powder, onion powder, salt, and pepper in a large mixing bowl. Mix well and form into 4 patties.
3. Place sweet potato waffle fries on a baking sheet, drizzle with olive oil, sprinkle with paprika, salt, and pepper, and toss to coat.
4. Bake fries in the preheated oven for 25-30 minutes, turning halfway through, until crispy.
5. While fries are baking, cook turkey patties on a grill or skillet over medium heat, 5-6 minutes per side, or until cooked through.
6. Assemble burgers on buns with lettuce, tomatoes, and your choice of condiments.

Nutritional Facts: (Per serving)

- ➢ Calories: 500
- ➢ Fat: 20g
- ➢ Protein: 30g
- ➢ Saturated Fat: 5g
- ➢ Carbohydrates: 55g
- ➢ Cholesterol: 120mg
- ➢ Dietary Fiber: 5g
- ➢ Sodium: 480mg
- ➢ Sugars: 8g

Elevate your brunch with the Turkey Burger and Sweet Potato Waffle Fries - a perfect ensemble of savory and sweet. Whether you're hosting a get-together or simply treating yourself, this dish epitomizes the essence of brunch: casual, delicious, and utterly satisfying. Dive into this modern classic and relish each bite.

Recipe 12: Sweet Mix Fruits Topping on Milk Tofu

Journey into a harmonious blend of textures and flavors with a Sweet Mix Fruits Topping on Milk Tofu. This delightful dish offers a gentle creaminess of tofu, crowned with a vibrant medley of fruits, making every bite a brunch-time revelation.

Servings: 4

Prepping Time: 15 minutes

Cook Time: 10 minutes (for the tofu)

Difficulty: Easy

Ingredients:

- 1 pack (14 oz.) of soft milk tofu or silken tofu, drained
- 1 cup diced strawberries & 1/2 cup blueberries
- 1/2 cup diced kiwi & 1/2 cup diced mango
- 2 tablespoons honey or maple syrup
- Fresh mint leaves for garnish

Step-by-Step Preparation:

1. Carefully remove the milk tofu from its package and place it on a serving dish.
2. Combine strawberries, blueberries, kiwi, and mango in a mixing bowl.
3. Drizzle the mixed fruits with honey or maple syrup and gently toss to coat.
4. Spoon the sweet fruit mixture over the milk tofu.
5. Garnish with fresh mint leaves for a burst of color and flavor.

Nutritional Facts: (Per serving)

- Calories: 130
- Protein: 5g
- Carbohydrates: 25g
- Dietary Fiber: 3g
- Sugars: 18g
- Fat: 2g
- Saturated Fat: 0.5g
- Cholesterol: 0mg
- Sodium: 15mg

Sweet Mix Fruits Topping on Milk Tofu invites you to experience brunch in a refreshingly new light. This dish, with its velvety tofu foundation and jubilant fruit cascade, is a testament to simplicity's brilliance. Ideal for those seeking a healthier yet utterly delectable option, this brunch bite is bound to win hearts.

Recipe 13: Fried Eggs in Tomato Sauce

Savor the delightful fusion of Fried Eggs in Tomato Sauce, a brunch dish that combines the comfort of sunny-side eggs with the tangy richness of tomatoes. Perfect for those who crave a hearty yet simple brunch escapade.

Servings: 4

Prepping Time: 10 minutes

Cook Time: 20 minutes

Difficulty: Easy

Ingredients:

- 4 large eggs
- 2 cups tomato sauce (homemade or store-bought)
- 2 cloves garlic, minced
- 1 small onion, finely chopped
- 2 tablespoons olive oil
- Salt and pepper to taste

- ✓ Fresh parsley or cilantro for garnish
- ✓ Crusty bread for serving

Step-by-Step Preparation:

1. In a skillet, heat olive oil over medium heat. Add onions and garlic, sautéing until translucent.
2. Pour the tomato sauce, season with salt and pepper, and let it simmer for 10 minutes.
3. Gently crack the eggs into the tomato sauce, spacing them evenly.
4. Cover the skillet and let the eggs cook for 7-10 minutes or until the whites are set but yolks remain runny.
5. Garnish with fresh parsley or cilantro.
6. Serve hot with crusty bread on the side.

Nutritional Facts: (Per serving)

- ➤ Calories: 190
- ➤ Protein: 8g
- ➤ Carbohydrates: 10g
- ➤ Dietary Fiber: 2g
- ➤ Sugars: 6g
- ➤ Fat: 13g
- ➤ Saturated Fat: 3g
- ➤ Cholesterol: 190mg
- ➤ Sodium: 650mg

Fried Eggs in Tomato Sauce is more than just a dish; it's a culinary experience. This brunch bite promises warmth, satisfaction, and a delightful burst of Mediterranean flair in every spoonful. Pair it with your favorite bread, and embark on a taste journey.

Recipe 14: Eggs Benedict

Indulge in the timeless classic of Eggs Benedict, a dish that masterfully layers delicately poached eggs atop tender ham, all crowned with a velvety hollandaise sauce. This brunch bite offers a symphony of flavors and textures, ensuring an unforgettable dining experience.

Servings: 4

Prepping Time: 20 minutes

Cook Time: 20 minutes

Difficulty: Intermediate

Ingredients:

- ✓ 4 large eggs
- ✓ 2 English muffins, halved
- ✓ 4 slices of ham or Canadian bacon
- ✓ 1 cup hollandaise sauce (homemade or store-bought)
- ✓ 2 tablespoons white vinegar

- ✓ Salt and pepper to taste
- ✓ Fresh parsley or chives for garnish
- ✓ Paprika or cayenne pepper (optional)

Step-by-Step Preparation:

1. Fill a deep skillet or saucepan with water, add white vinegar, and bring to a gentle simmer.
2. Crack each egg into a small bowl and carefully slide it into the simmering water. Poach for 3-4 minutes or until the whites are set but yolks remain runny.
3. Toast the English muffins until golden brown.
4. Place a slice of ham or Canadian bacon on each muffin half.
5. Using a slotted spoon, place a poached egg on each muffin.
6. Generously spoon hollandaise sauce over the eggs.
7. Season with salt, pepper, and optional paprika or cayenne. Garnish with fresh parsley or chives.

Nutritional Facts: (Per serving)

- ➢ Calories: 320
- ➢ Protein: 16g
- ➢ Carbohydrates: 25g
- ➢ Dietary Fiber: 2g
- ➢ Sugars: 3g
- ➢ Fat: 18g
- ➢ Saturated Fat: 9g
- ➢ Cholesterol: 220mg
- ➢ Sodium: 680mg

Eggs Benedict isn't just brunch; it's a celebration on a plate. As you cut into the poached egg and watch the yolk cascade over the muffin, it's a reminder of life's simple yet profound pleasures. Elevate your brunch gatherings or treat yourself with this elegant, evergreen dish that's been charming palates for decades.

Recipe 15: Berry Bread Pudding with Mulberries

Dive into the sweet embrace of Berry Bread Pudding with Mulberries, a delightful twist on a classic brunch favorite. This dish combines the soft textures of bread pudding with the tartness of berries, crowned by the unique flavor of mulberries, for an unforgettable taste sensation.

Servings: 6

Prepping Time: 15 minutes

Cook Time: 45 minutes

Difficulty: Easy

Ingredients:

- ✓ 6 cups of day-old bread, cubed
- ✓ 2 cups of mixed berries (like blueberries, raspberries, and strawberries)
- ✓ 1 cup fresh mulberries
- ✓ 4 large eggs

- ✓ 2 cups milk
- ✓ 1 cup granulated sugar
- ✓ 1 teaspoon vanilla extract
- ✓ 1/2 teaspoon cinnamon
- ✓ Powdered sugar for garnish (optional)

Step-by-Step Preparation:

1. Preheat oven to 350°F (175°C).
2. Whisk together eggs, milk, granulated sugar, vanilla extract, and cinnamon in a large mixing bowl.
3. Fold in the bread cubes, ensuring each piece is well-coated.
4. Gently stir in the mixed berries.
5. Pour the mixture into a greased baking dish and evenly sprinkle mulberries.
6. Bake for 40-45 minutes or until the top is golden and the center is set.
7. Let cool slightly, then dust with powdered sugar if desired.

Nutritional Facts: (Per serving)

- ➢ Calories: 290
- ➢ Protein: 8g
- ➢ Carbohydrates: 55g
- ➢ Dietary Fiber: 3g
- ➢ Sugars: 35g
- ➢ Fat: 6g
- ➢ Saturated Fat: 2.5g
- ➢ Cholesterol: 120mg
- ➢ Sodium: 230mg

Berry Bread Pudding with Mulberries encapsulates the essence of a perfect brunch: cozy, flavorful, and full of surprises. This dish explores textures and tastes, with every bite promising the warmth of bread pudding and the zest of summer berries. Ideal for family brunches or solo indulgences, it's a recipe that beckons one to revisit time and time.

Recipe 16: Bliss Avocado-Baked Egg on Toast

Embrace a fusion of creamy avocado and perfectly baked eggs with the Bliss Avocado-Baked Egg on Toast. This brunch delicacy delivers a burst of nutrition and flavor, marrying the buttery texture of avocado with the rich goodness of a baked egg for an elevated morning experience.

Servings: 4

Prepping Time: 10 minutes

Cook Time: 15 minutes

Difficulty: Easy

Ingredients:

- ✓ 4 slices of your preferred bread
- ✓ 2 ripe avocados, halved and pitted
- ✓ 4 large eggs
- ✓ Salt and pepper to taste
- ✓ 1 tablespoon chopped chives
- ✓ 1/4 teaspoon red chili flakes (optional)

- ✓ Olive oil for drizzling

Step-by-Step Preparation:

1. Preheat the oven to 425°F (220°C).
2. Carve out a small space in each avocado half to ensure it can snugly fit an egg.
3. Place avocados on a baking sheet.
4. Carefully crack an egg into each avocado half.
5. Season with salt and pepper.
6. Bake in the oven for 12-15 minutes or until the egg whites are set.
7. Toast bread slices till they're golden brown.
8. Place each avocado egg on a piece of toast.
9. Garnish with chives, red chili flakes, and a drizzle of olive oil.

Nutritional Facts: (Per serving)

- ➢ Calories: 270
- ➢ Protein: 9g
- ➢ Carbohydrates: 20g
- ➢ Dietary Fiber: 7g
- ➢ Sugars: 3g
- ➢ Fat: 18g
- ➢ Saturated Fat: 3.5g
- ➢ Cholesterol: 185mg
- ➢ Sodium: 210mg

Every bite of the Bliss Avocado-Baked Egg on Toast is a journey through layers of taste and texture, bringing forth a harmony of simple ingredients. Ideal for those seeking a wholesome yet gourmet brunch experience, this dish is a testament to the magic of pairing classic ingredients in new, delightful ways.

Recipe 17: Mini Cheese Burger Buns

Bite into a world of flavor with the Mini Cheese Burger Buns, perfect for brunches or midday cravings. These little delights combine the charm of sliders with the richness of cheese, offering an irresistible treat for both the eyes and the palate.

Servings: 8

Prepping Time: 15 minutes

Cook Time: 20 minutes

Difficulty: Medium

Ingredients:

- 8 mini burger buns & 1-pound ground beef
- 8 slices of cheddar cheese & Salt and pepper to taste
- 1/2 cup diced onions & 2 tablespoons ketchup
- 1 tablespoon mustard & Lettuce leaves for garnish
- 2 tomatoes, sliced

Step-by-Step Preparation:

1. Preheat the grill or stovetop pan over medium heat.
2. Season the ground beef with salt and pepper, then form into 8 small patties.
3. Grill patties for about 3 minutes on each side or until they reach the desired doneness.
4. Place a slice of cheese on each cake for a minute before removing it from the grill, allowing it to melt.
5. Slice open the mini burger buns and spread ketchup on one side and mustard on the other.
6. Assemble the burger by placing the patty on the bun, followed by onions, a tomato slice, and lettuce.
7. Cap it with the top half of the bun.

Nutritional Facts: (Per serving)

- Calories: 320
- Protein: 17g
- Carbohydrates: 20g
- Dietary Fiber: 1g
- Sugars: 3g
- Fat: 18g
- Saturated Fat: 7g
- Cholesterol: 55mg
- Sodium: 420mg

The Mini Cheese Burger Buns offer a delightful twist to traditional brunch fare. Each bite is packed with the classic flavors of a cheeseburger but presented in a bite-sized format, perfect for gatherings or solo indulgences. With every taste, be transported to a world where comfort food meets gourmet presentation. Enjoy!

Recipe 18: Frittata with Grilled Summer Vegetables Baked

Unveil the magic of summer with the Frittata with Grilled Summer Vegetables Baked dish. This brunch delight embraces the essence of sun-kissed vegetables, enveloped in a savory egg mixture, resulting in a baked delicacy that genuinely captures the season's spirit.

Servings: 6

Prepping Time: 20 minutes

Cook Time: 25 minutes

Difficulty: Medium

Ingredients:

- ✓ 8 large eggs & 1/4 cup milk & Salt and pepper to taste
- ✓ 1 zucchini, sliced & 1 yellow bell pepper, diced
- ✓ 1 red onion, thinly sliced & 1 cup cherry tomatoes, halved
- ✓ 2 tablespoons olive oil

- ✓ 1/2 cup grated parmesan cheese
- ✓ Fresh basil leaves for garnish

Step-by-Step Preparation:

1. Preheat the grill to medium-high heat and oven to 375°F (190°C).
2. Toss the zucchini, bell pepper, onion, and cherry tomatoes in olive oil, salt, and pepper.
3. Grill the vegetables until tender and slightly charred.
4. Whisk together the eggs, milk, salt, pepper, and half of the parmesan cheese in a mixing bowl.
5. Stir in the grilled vegetables.
6. Pour the mixture into a greased baking dish.
7. Sprinkle with the remaining parmesan cheese.
8. Bake for about 25 minutes or until set.
9. Garnish with fresh basil leaves before serving.

Nutritional Facts: (Per serving)

- ➢ Calories: 180
- ➢ Protein: 11g
- ➢ Carbohydrates: 8g
- ➢ Dietary Fiber: 2g
- ➢ Sugars: 4g
- ➢ Fat: 12g
- ➢ Saturated Fat: 4g
- ➢ Cholesterol: 245mg
- ➢ Sodium: 250mg

Let your senses be tantalized by the Frittata with Grilled Summer Vegetables Baked dish. Perfect for a sunny brunch, this plate merges the zest of fresh produce with the heartiness of eggs. With each bite, you're transported to a breezy summer day, making it the perfect dish to share or savor solo. Celebrate the flavors of summer in style!

Recipe 19: Cheesecake for Agar-Agar with Cherries and Almonds

Delight in the fusion of classic cheesecake with a twist in the "Cheesecake for Agar-Agar with Cherries and Almonds." This brunch bite marries the creaminess of cheesecake with the gelatinous charm of agar-agar, while cherries and almonds introduce a burst of flavor and crunch.

Servings: 8

Prepping Time: 25 minutes

Cook Time: 40 minutes

Difficulty: Medium

Ingredients:

- ✓ 1 1/2 cups graham cracker crumbs
- ✓ 6 tablespoons unsalted butter, melted
- ✓ 16 oz cream cheese, softened & 3/4 cup sugar
- ✓ 2 teaspoons vanilla extract

- ✓ 2 tablespoons agar-agar powder & 1/2 cup boiling water
- ✓ 1 cup cherries, pitted and halved
- ✓ 1/2 cup roasted almonds, chopped & Zest of 1 lemon

Step-by-Step Preparation:

1. Preheat oven to 325°F (165°C).
2. Mix graham cracker crumbs and melted butter. Press onto the bottom of a springform pan to form a crust.
3. Beat cream cheese, sugar, and vanilla until smooth.
4. Dissolve agar-agar in boiling water and gradually blend into the cream cheese mixture.
5. Fold in cherries, almonds, and lemon zest.
6. Pour over the crust and spread evenly.
7. Bake for 40 minutes or until set.
8. Allow to cool, then refrigerate for at least 4 hours before serving.

Nutritional Facts: (Per serving)

- ➢ Calories: 385
- ➢ Protein: 6g
- ➢ Carbohydrates: 32g
- ➢ Dietary Fiber: 2g
- ➢ Sugars: 20g
- ➢ Fat: 26g
- ➢ Saturated Fat: 14g
- ➢ Cholesterol: 80mg
- ➢ Sodium: 280

The Cheesecake for Agar-Agar with Cherries and Almonds is a sumptuous amalgamation of diverse textures and tastes. Perfect for a decadent brunch, this cheesecake guarantees a delightful mouthfeel and flavor sensation with every bite. Elevate your brunch experience and immerse yourself in this delectable treat!

Recipe 20: Healthy Match Bliss Energy Balls with Dates Hemp and Nuts

Energize your brunch moments with the "Healthy Match Bliss Energy Balls with Dates, Hemp, and Nuts." These bite-sized delights not only satiate your sweet cravings but also fuel your day with the goodness of superfoods.

Servings: 12

Prepping Time: 15 minutes

Cook Time: 0 minutes (No-bake)

Difficulty: Easy

Ingredients:

- ✓ 1 cup Medjool dates, pitted
- ✓ 2 tablespoons match powder
- ✓ 1/2 cup hemp seeds
- ✓ 1/2 cup mixed nuts (almonds, walnuts, and cashews)
- ✓ 1 teaspoon vanilla extract & A pinch of sea salt

Step-by-Step Preparation:

1. In a food processor, blend the dates until smooth.
2. Add match powder, hemp seeds, mixed nuts, vanilla extract, and sea salt. Process until well combined.
3. Using your hands, form the mixture into small balls.
4. Place the balls on a tray lined with parchment paper.
5. Refrigerate for 1-2 hours or until firm.

Nutritional Facts: (Per serving)

- Calories: 115
- Protein: 3g
- Carbohydrates: 18g
- Dietary Fiber: 2g
- Sugars: 15g
- Fat: 5g
- Saturated Fat: 0.5g
- Sodium: 5mg

The Healthy Match Bliss Energy Balls are the quintessential guilt-free treat, perfect for brunch or whenever you need a quick energy boost. These balls are a healthy harmony of flavors and nutrients, sure to please your palate and body.

Chapter 03: Lunch Lifters

Recipe 21: Power Salad with Black Beans Avocado and Cooked White Rice

Supercharge your lunch hours with the "Power Salad with Black Beans, Avocado, and Cooked White Rice." A perfect amalgamation of protein, healthy fats, and carbs, this salad promises to be both deliciously satisfying and nutritionally uplifting for the midday slump.

Servings: 4

Prepping Time: 10 minutes

Cook Time: 20 minutes (for rice if not pre-cooked)

Difficulty: Easy

Ingredients:

- 1 cup cooked white rice
- 1 can black beans, drained and rinsed

- ✓ 1 ripe avocado, sliced
- ✓ 1 red bell pepper, diced
- ✓ 2 green onions, chopped
- ✓ Juice of 1 lime
- ✓ 2 tablespoons olive oil
- ✓ Salt and pepper, to taste
- ✓ Fresh cilantro for garnish

Step-by-Step Preparation:

1. Combine rice, black beans, avocado slices, red bell pepper, and green onions in a large mixing bowl.
2. Whisk together lime juice, olive oil, salt, and pepper in a separate bowl to create the dressing.
3. Drizzle the sauce over the salad and toss gently to mix.
4. Garnish with fresh cilantro.
5. Serve chilled or at room temperature.

Nutritional Facts: (Per serving)

- ➢ Calories: 290
- ➢ Protein: 9g
- ➢ Carbohydrates: 42g
- ➢ Dietary Fiber: 9g
- ➢ Sugars: 2g
- ➢ Fat: 11g
- ➢ Saturated Fat: 1.5g
- ➢ Sodium: 55mg

The Power Salad embodies everything a Lunch Lifter dish should be - wholesome, delicious, and easy to assemble. Its rich ingredients not only tantalize the taste buds but also ensure sustained energy throughout the day, making it a staple for those seeking both flavor and function in their midday meal.

Recipe 22: Teriyaki Tofu Rice Bowl

Dive into the delightful fusion of flavors with the Teriyaki Tofu Rice Bowl. A classic oriental dish reimagined as a brunch special; it's the perfect blend of savory teriyaki and tender tofu atop a bed of fluffy rice.

Servings: 4

Prepping Time: 15 minutes

Cook Time: 20 minutes

Difficulty: Medium

Ingredients:

- ✓ 1 block of firm tofu, cubed
- ✓ 2 cups jasmine or basmati rice
- ✓ 1/4 cup teriyaki sauce
- ✓ 1 tablespoon sesame oil
- ✓ 1 red bell pepper, thinly sliced

- ✓ 2 green onions, chopped
- ✓ 1 tablespoon sesame seeds
- ✓ 1 tablespoon vegetable oil for frying

Step-by-Step Preparation:

1. Cook the rice according to package instructions and set aside.
2. Heat vegetable oil in a pan and fry tofu cubes until golden brown.
3. Add sesame oil and teriyaki sauce to the pan, coating the tofu evenly.
4. Serve tofu over a rice bowl, garnishing with red bell pepper slices, green onions, and a sprinkle of sesame seeds.

Nutritional Facts: (Per serving)

- ➢ Calories: 350
- ➢ Protein: 15g
- ➢ Carbohydrates: 50g
- ➢ Dietary Fiber: 3g
- ➢ Sugars: 6g
- ➢ Fat: 10g
- ➢ Saturated Fat: 1g
- ➢ Sodium: 800mg

The Teriyaki Tofu Rice Bowl brings an Asian touch to your brunch spread, ensuring every bite has a burst of flavors. It's a delicious nod to classic Asian cuisine, effortlessly fitting into a relaxed brunch atmosphere.

Recipe 23: Quinoa with Vegetables

Indulge in the wholesome goodness of "Quinoa with Vegetables," a delightful medley serving taste and nutrition on your brunch table. This dish promises a hearty experience, with fluffy quinoa grains mingling with garden-fresh vegetables.

Servings: 4

Prepping Time: 10 minutes

Cook Time: 20 minutes

Difficulty: Easy

Ingredients:

- ✓ 1 cup quinoa
- ✓ 2 cups vegetable broth or water
- ✓ 1 bell pepper, diced
- ✓ 1 zucchini, diced
- ✓ 1 carrot, diced
- ✓ 2 tablespoons olive oil

- ✓ 2 garlic cloves, minced
- ✓ Salt and pepper, to taste
- ✓ Fresh parsley, chopped for garnish

Step-by-Step Preparation:

1. Rinse quinoa thoroughly and drain.
2. In a pot, bring vegetable broth or water to a boil. Add quinoa, cover, and simmer for 15 minutes or until cooked.
3. Heat olive oil and sauté garlic, bell pepper, zucchini, and carrot in a skillet until tender.
4. Fluff-cooked quinoa with a fork and mix with the sautéed vegetables. Season with salt and pepper.
5. Garnish with fresh parsley before serving.

Nutritional Facts: (Per serving)

- ➢ Calories: 210
- ➢ Protein: 8g
- ➢ Carbohydrates: 36g
- ➢ Dietary Fiber: 4g
- ➢ Sugars: 3g
- ➢ Fat: 5g
- ➢ Saturated Fat: 0.7g
- ➢ Sodium: 480mg

"Quinoa with Vegetables" is a true brunch champion, offering a savory, nutritious, and satisfying ensemble. A perfect blend of textures and flavors, it's sure to become a regular on your brunch rotation.

Recipe 24: Delicious Salad with Anchovies and Battered Cheese

Dive into the bold flavors of "Delicious Salad with Anchovies and Battered Cheese," a dish that combines the saltiness of anchovies with the rich creaminess of cheese. This salad is an exciting twist on the classic brunch offering, sure to captivate your palate.

Servings: 4

Prepping Time: 15 minutes

Cook Time: 10 minutes

Difficulty: Medium

Ingredients:

- 8 anchovy fillets
- 200g cheese (like mozzarella or halloumi), sliced and battered
- Mixed salad greens
- 2 eggs, beaten (for battering)

- ✓ 1 cup breadcrumbs (for battering)
- ✓ Olive oil for frying
- ✓ 1 lemon, zest and juice
- ✓ Salt and pepper, to taste

Step-by-Step Preparation:

1. Dredge the cheese slices in beaten eggs, then coat with breadcrumbs.
2. In a skillet, heat olive oil and fry the battered cheese until golden brown on both sides. Drain on paper towels.
3. Arrange salad greens on plates, and place anchovy fillets and fried cheese slices on top.
4. Drizzle with lemon zest and juice, then season with salt and pepper.

Nutritional Facts: (Per serving)

- ➢ Calories: 310
- ➢ Protein: 16g
- ➢ Carbohydrates: 20g
- ➢ Dietary Fiber: 2g
- ➢ Sugars: 3g
- ➢ Fat: 20g
- ➢ Saturated Fat: 7g
- ➢ Sodium: 750mg

"Delicious Salad with Anchovies and Battered Cheese" promises a gustatory journey with every bite. Perfect for those looking to elevate their brunch experience, this dish effortlessly marries contrasting flavors into a cohesive, delightful meal.

Recipe 25: Vegan Pasta with Carrots Celery and Fresh Pesto Sauce

Dive into a delectable plate of "Vegan Pasta with Carrots, Celery, and Fresh Pesto Sauce." This dish offers the vibrant taste of fresh vegetables and aromatic pesto, ensuring a delightful brunch option for vegans and pasta lovers.

Servings: 4

Prepping Time: 20 minutes

Cook Time: 15 minutes

Difficulty: Easy

Ingredients:

- ✓ 400g vegan pasta of choice
- ✓ 2 medium carrots, julienned
- ✓ 2 stalks of celery (celery), chopped
- ✓ 1 cup fresh pesto sauce

- ✓ 2 tbsp olive oil
- ✓ 3 garlic cloves, minced
- ✓ Salt and pepper, to taste
- ✓ Fresh basil for garnish

Step-by-Step Preparation:

1. Boil pasta according to package instructions until al dente. Drain and set aside.
2. In a skillet, heat olive oil and sauté garlic until fragrant. Add julienned carrots and chopped celery. Cook until slightly tender.
3. Add the cooked pasta to the skillet and stir in the fresh pesto sauce.
4. Season with salt and pepper. Serve hot, garnished with fresh basil.

Nutritional Facts: (Per serving)

- ➢ Calories: 450
- ➢ Protein: 12g
- ➢ Carbohydrates: 65g
- ➢ Dietary Fiber: 5g
- ➢ Sugars: 4g
- ➢ Fat: 15g
- ➢ Saturated Fat: 2g
- ➢ Sodium: 200mg

The "Vegan Pasta with Carrots, Celeri, and Fresh Pesto Sauce" is a testament to how vegan dishes can be as rich and fulfilling as their non-vegan counterparts. Perfect for a vibrant brunch or a light dinner, every forkful promises a taste of Italian summer.

Recipe 26: Golden Lentil Spinach Soup

Warm up with a comforting bowl of "Golden Lentil Spinach Soup." A wholesome blend of nutritious lentils and fresh spinach creates a hearty dish that revitalizes and nourishes, making it the ultimate brunch choice for those looking for a healthful treat.

Servings: 4

Prepping Time: 15 minutes

Cook Time: 30 minutes

Difficulty: Easy

Ingredients:

- 1 cup dried lentils, rinsed and drained
- 3 cups fresh spinach, chopped
- 1 onion, diced
- 2 garlic cloves, minced
- 4 cups vegetable broth

- ✓ 1 tsp turmeric powder
- ✓ 1/2 tsp ground cumin
- ✓ 1 tbsp olive oil
- ✓ Salt and pepper, to taste
- ✓ Lemon wedges for serving

Step-by-Step Preparation:

1. In a pot, heat olive oil and sauté onion and garlic until translucent.
2. Add the lentils, turmeric, and cumin, stirring for a few minutes.
3. Pour in the vegetable broth and bring to a boil. Reduce heat and let simmer for 25 minutes.
4. Stir in the chopped spinach, cooking until wilted.
5. Season with salt and pepper. Serve hot with a squeeze of lemon.

Nutritional Facts: (Per serving)

- ➢ Calories: 210
- ➢ Protein: 13g
- ➢ Carbohydrates: 35g
- ➢ Dietary Fiber: 15g
- ➢ Sugars: 3g
- ➢ Fat: 3g
- ➢ Saturated Fat: 0.5g
- ➢ Sodium: 600mg

The "Golden Lentil Spinach Soup" is a testament to simplicity at its best. Whether enjoyed on a brisk morning or as a mid-day refresher, this soup brings a perfect balance of flavors and nutrients that cater to both taste buds and well-being. Dive in!

Recipe 27: Healthy Asian Chicken Lettuce Wrap with Carrots

Indulge in the refreshing burst of flavors with "Healthy Asian Chicken Lettuce Wrap with Carrots." This low-carb delight combines the savory goodness of chicken with the crispiness of lettuce and carrots, making it an irresistible brunch bite.

Servings: 4

Prepping Time: 20 minutes

Cook Time: 15 minutes

Difficulty: Moderate

Ingredients:

- ✓ 500g ground chicken
- ✓ 8 large lettuce leaves, washed and dried
- ✓ 2 carrots, julienned
- ✓ 2 green onions, sliced

- ✓ 3 tbsp soy sauce
- ✓ 1 tbsp sesame oil
- ✓ 2 garlic cloves, minced
- ✓ 1 tsp ginger, grated
- ✓ 1 tbsp honey
- ✓ Crushed peanuts (optional for garnish)
- ✓ Fresh cilantro, chopped (for garnish)

Step-by-Step Preparation:

1. In a skillet, heat sesame oil and sauté garlic and ginger until fragrant.
2. Add the ground chicken and cook until browned.
3. Stir in the soy sauce and honey, cooking for 5 minutes.
4. Place a generous amount of the chicken mixture onto each lettuce leaf.
5. Top with julienned carrots, green onions, crushed peanuts, and cilantro.
6. Serve immediately and enjoy!

Nutritional Facts: (Per serving)

- ➢ Calories: 250
- ➢ Protein: 20g
- ➢ Carbohydrates: 12g
- ➢ Dietary Fiber: 2g
- ➢ Sugars: 7g
- ➢ Fat: 13g
- ➢ Saturated Fat: 3g
- ➢ Sodium: 700mg

The "Healthy Asian Chicken Lettuce Wrap with Carrots" epitomizes flavor and health in every bite. Perfect for those who crave an Asian twist to their brunch, this dish promises satisfaction without the guilt. Embrace a flavorful journey with each wrap!

Recipe 28: Roast Beef Rocket and Horseradish Sandwich

Delve into savory brunches with the "Roast Beef, Rocket, and Horseradish Sandwich." This classic combination promises a symphony of flavors, marrying the tender roast beef with the peppery rocket and the fiery kick of horseradish.

Servings: 4

Prepping Time: 15 minutes

Cook Time: Nil (assuming pre-cooked roast beef)

Difficulty: Easy

Ingredients:

- ✓ 8 slices of whole grain bread
- ✓ 400g sliced roast beef
- ✓ 2 cups rocket (arugula) leaves, washed and dried
- ✓ 4 tbsp horseradish sauce
- ✓ 1 red onion, thinly sliced

- ✓ Salt and pepper, to taste
- ✓ 2 tbsp olive oil

Step-by-Step Preparation:

1. Lay out the slices of bread on a flat surface.
2. Evenly spread the horseradish sauce on each piece.
3. Layer with cuts of roast beef, followed by rocket leaves.
4. Add slices of red onion on top and sprinkle with salt and pepper.
5. Drizzle a bit of olive oil over each sandwich for added flavor.
6. Top with another piece of bread and serve immediately.

Nutritional Facts: (Per serving)

- Calories: 320
- Protein: 28g
- Carbohydrates: 25g
- Dietary Fiber: 4g
- Sugars: 4g
- Fat: 12g
- Saturated Fat: 3g
- Sodium: 580mg

The "Roast Beef, Rocket, and Horseradish Sandwich" epitomizes brunch perfection, offering a hearty yet sophisticated palate. Perfect for those seeking an elevated sandwich experience, every bite ensures balanced, delectable flavors. Dive in and elevate your brunch game!

Recipe 29: Grilled Chicken Salad

Indulge in the fresh and flavorsome "Grilled Chicken Salad," an exquisite blend of succulent chicken, crisp veggies, and an irresistible dressing. This delightful dish is a brunch favorite, ensuring a light yet fulfilling meal that keeps you energized throughout the day.

Servings: 4

Prepping Time: 20 minutes

Cook Time: 10 minutes

Difficulty: Easy

Ingredients:

- 4 boneless chicken breasts
- 1 cup cherry tomatoes, halved
- 4 cups mixed salad greens
- 1 cucumber, sliced
- 1/2 red onion, thinly sliced

- ✓ 1/4 cup feta cheese, crumbled
- ✓ 2 tbsp olive oil
- ✓ Salt and pepper, to taste
- ✓ 1/4 cup balsamic vinaigrette dressing

Step-by-Step Preparation:

1. Preheat the grill to medium heat.
2. Rub chicken breasts with olive oil, salt, and pepper.
3. Grill chicken for 5 minutes on each side or until fully cooked. Remove and let it rest.
4. Slice grilled chicken into thin strips.
5. Combine salad greens, cherry tomatoes, cucumber, and onion in a large bowl.
6. Top the salad with grilled chicken strips and crumbled feta cheese.
7. Drizzle balsamic vinaigrette dressing over the salad before serving.

Nutritional Facts: (Per serving)

- ➤ Calories: 275
- ➤ Protein: 30g
- ➤ Carbohydrates: 8g
- ➤ Dietary Fiber: 2g
- ➤ Sugars: 4g
- ➤ Fat: 12g
- ➤ Saturated Fat: 3.5g
- ➤ Sodium: 420m

The "Grilled Chicken Salad" is more than just a meal; it's an experience of freshness and flavor. Perfectly charred chicken on a bed of crunchy vegetables ensures every bite is a treat. This dish is nutritious and delicious to your taste buds, making brunch both indulgent and wholesome. Enjoy!

Recipe 30: Delicious Veggie Bowl with Cucumber

Dive into the refreshing taste of the "Delicious Veggie Bowl with Cucumber," a medley of colorful vegetables complemented by the cool crunch of cucumber. This wholesome dish epitomizes a nourishing brunch bite, promising flavor and nutrition in every scoop.

Servings: 4

Prepping Time: 15 minutes

Cook Time: 0 minutes

Difficulty: Easy

Ingredients:

- 2 large cucumbers, sliced
- 1 cup cherry tomatoes, halved
- 1 red bell pepper, diced
- 1/2 red onion, thinly sliced

- ✓ 1 cup shredded purple cabbage
- ✓ 1 carrot, julienned
- ✓ 2 tbsp sesame seeds
- ✓ Fresh coriander, chopped (for garnish)
- ✓ Lemon-tahini dressing

Step-by-Step Preparation:

1. Combine cucumbers, cherry tomatoes, bell pepper, red onion, purple cabbage, and carrot in a large mixing bowl.
2. Toss the vegetables gently to mix well.
3. Transfer the mixed vegetables to serving bowls.
4. Drizzle with lemon-tahini dressing.
5. Sprinkle sesame seeds on top.
6. Garnish with chopped coriander before serving.

Nutritional Facts: (Per serving)

- ➤ Calories: 80
- ➤ Protein: 2g
- ➤ Carbohydrates: 16g
- ➤ Dietary Fiber: 4g
- ➤ Sugars: 8g
- ➤ Fat: 0.5g
- ➤ Sodium: 20mg

The "Delicious Veggie Bowl with Cucumber" offers a delightful crunch and burst of flavors. Perfect for a light yet satisfying brunch, it's a testament to how simple ingredients can create an indulgent and health-promoting meal. Enjoy this bowl of veggie goodness, and keep your day going strong!

Chapter 04: Afternoon Energizers

Recipe 31: Energy Candy Balls Made of Chickpeas Dates and Pistachios

Dive into unconventional delights with "Energy Candy Balls Made of Chickpeas, Dates, and Pistachios." These bite-sized powerhouses fuse chickpeas' nutty undertones with dates' natural sweetness, uplifted by crunchy pistachios. Ideal for a mid-morning snack or brunch bite, they're sure to surprise and satisfy.

Servings: 12 balls

Prepping Time: 10 minutes

Cook Time: 0 minutes (requires chilling)

Difficulty: Easy

Ingredients:

- ✓ 1 cup cooked chickpeas, drained and rinsed
- ✓ 10 Medrol dates, pitted

- ✓ 1/2 cup shelled pistachios
- ✓ 1 tsp vanilla extract
- ✓ A pinch of salt
- ✓ Shredded coconut (for rolling, optional)

Step-by-Step Preparation:

1. Blend chickpeas, dates, pistachios, vanilla extract, and salt in a food processor until a sticky mixture form.
2. Scoop out tablespoon-sized amounts and roll into balls using your hands.
3. Roll the balls in shredded coconut for added texture and flavor if desired.
4. Chill in the refrigerator for at least an hour before serving.

Nutritional Facts: (Per serving)

- ➢ Calories: 95
- ➢ Protein: 3g
- ➢ Carbohydrates: 18g
- ➢ Dietary Fiber: 3g
- ➢ Sugars: 12g
- ➢ Fat: 2g
- ➢ Sodium: 5mg

"Energy Candy Balls Made of Chickpeas, Dates, and Pistachios" are a treat for your taste buds and a boon for energy seekers. These delightful morsels, bursting with flavor and nutrition, make for a perfect brunch bite or a pick-me-up anytime during the day. Indulge guilt-free and stay energized!

Recipe 32: Chocolate Vegan Brownie Cake

Experience the decadence of the "Chocolate Vegan Brownie Cake," an irresistible treat that even non-vegans will adore. This sumptuous dessert combines rich cocoa with a tender crumb, perfect for brunch or any chocolate-craving moment.

Servings: 12 pieces

Prepping Time: 15 minutes

Cook Time: 25 minutes

Difficulty: Moderate

Ingredients:

- ✓ 2 cups all-purpose flour & 1 cup unsweetened cocoa powder
- ✓ 1 1/2 cups coconut sugar or brown sugar
- ✓ 1 tsp baking powder & 1/2 tsp baking soda
- ✓ 1/4 tsp salt & 1 cup almond milk or any plant-based milk
- ✓ 1/2 cup coconut oil, melted & 1 tsp vanilla extract

- ✓ 1/2 cup vegan chocolate chips (optional)

Step-by-Step Preparation:

1. Preheat oven to 350°F (175°C) and grease a 9x9-inch baking pan.
2. Whisk together flour, cocoa powder, sugar, baking powder, baking powder, baking soda, and salt in a large bowl.
3. Stir in almond milk, melted coconut oil, and vanilla until combined.
4. Fold in vegan chocolate chips if using.
5. Pour the batter into the prepared pan and smooth the top.
6. Bake for 25 minutes or until a toothpick comes out with a few crumbs.
7. Allow to cool before slicing.

Nutritional Facts: (Per serving)

- ➢ Calories: 265
- ➢ Protein: 4g
- ➢ Carbohydrates: 42g
- ➢ Dietary Fiber: 3g
- ➢ Sugars: 22g
- ➢ Fat: 11g
- ➢ Sodium: 150mg

The "Chocolate Vegan Brownie Cake" promises a delightful experience for anyone seeking indulgence without compromise. Perfectly paired with a hot coffee or tea, this cake elevates your brunch spread, making it a sure shot crowd-pleaser. Enjoy every chocolatey bite!

Recipe 33: Raw Organic Homemade Trail Mix with Nuts and Fruits

Dive into a crunchy, nutritious blend with "Raw Organic Homemade Trail Mix with Nuts and Fruits." This handpicked mix of nature's best offers an energy-boosting snack perfect for brunch, hikes, or any on-the-go occasion. With zero cooking involved, it's all about simplicity and health combined.

Servings: 10 portions

Prepping Time: 10 minutes

Cook Time: None

Difficulty: Easy

Ingredients:

- ✓ 1 cup raw almonds
- ✓ 1 cup raw walnuts
- ✓ 1/2 cup dried cranberries
- ✓ 1/2 cup organic raisins
- ✓ 1/2 cup dried apricots, chopped

- ✓ 1/4 cup pumpkin seeds
- ✓ 1/4 cup sunflower seeds
- ✓ 1/4 cup unsweetened coconut flakes

Step-by-Step Preparation:

1. Combine almonds, walnuts, cranberries, raisins, and apricots in a large mixing bowl.
2. Add in the pumpkin seeds, sunflower seeds, and coconut flakes.
3. Mix well until all ingredients are evenly distributed.
4. Store in an airtight container in a cool and dry place.

Nutritional Facts: (Per serving)

- ➢ Calories: 210
- ➢ Protein: 6g
- ➢ Carbohydrates: 23g
- ➢ Dietary Fiber: 4g
- ➢ Sugars: 14g
- ➢ Fat: 12g
- ➢ Sodium: 5mg

This "Raw Organic Homemade Trail Mix with Nuts and Fruits" provides a naturally sweet and savory bite, fueling your day with essential nutrients. Keep a stash in your bag for a ready energy boost. Perfect for brunch spreads or a quick snack, this mix showcases the goodness of raw, organic ingredients. Enjoy!

Recipe 34: Nachos with Green Guacamole

Dive into a fiesta of flavors with "Nachos with Green Guacamole." These crispy chips and creamy avocado goodness make for an irresistible brunch delight. Whether you're entertaining guests or enjoying a cozy weekend, this dish will leave everyone asking for more.

Servings: 4

Prepping Time: 15 minutes

Cook Time: 10 minutes

Difficulty: Easy

Ingredients:

- ✓ 200g tortilla chips
- ✓ 2 ripe avocados, peeled and pitted
- ✓ 1 lime, juiced
- ✓ 1 small red onion, finely chopped
- ✓ 1 jalapeño, deseeded and minced

- ✓ 2 tablespoons fresh cilantro, chopped
- ✓ Salt, to taste
- ✓ 1 tomato, diced (optional)

Step-by-Step Preparation:

1. In a bowl, mash the avocados until smooth.
2. Mix in lime juice, red onion, jalapeño, cilantro, and salt.
3. If preferred, fold in the diced tomato.
4. Preheat oven to 180°C (350°F). Spread tortilla chips on a baking tray and bake for 5-7 minutes until crispy.
5. Serve chips with freshly made guacamole.

Nutritional Facts: (Per serving)

- ➤ Calories: 320
- ➤ Protein: 5g
- ➤ Carbohydrates: 30g
- ➤ Dietary Fiber: 8g
- ➤ Sugars: 2g
- ➤ Fat: 21g
- ➤ Sodium: 210mg

"Nachos with Green Guacamole" brings a combination of divine textures and flavors. Enjoy the satisfying crunch of nachos paired with the smooth richness of guacamole. Perfect for brunch, gatherings, or even a solo treat – this dish is a celebration in every bite. Enjoy your fiesta!

Recipe 35: Delicious Roasted Almonds and Large Pieces

Indulge in the simple yet elegant "Delicious Roasted Almonds and Large Pieces." Perfectly roasted to bring out their natural flavors, these almonds make an excellent snack or addition to any brunch spread, offering taste and nutrition in every bite.

Servings: 6

Prepping Time: 5 minutes

Cook Time: 15 minutes

Difficulty: Easy

Ingredients:

- 2 cups raw almonds
- 2 tablespoons olive oil or melted coconut oil
- 1 teaspoon sea salt (or to taste)
- Optional: 1 teaspoon rosemary or preferred seasoning

Step-by-Step Preparation:

1. Preheat the oven to 180°C (350°F).
2. In a mixing bowl, combine almonds and oil, ensuring all nuts are coated.
3. Sprinkle salt and optional seasoning, mixing well.
4. Spread the almonds in a single layer on a baking sheet.
5. Roast in the oven for 12-15 minutes, stirring occasionally, until golden.
6. Let cool before serving.

Nutritional Facts: (Per serving)

- Calories: 210
- Protein: 8g
- Carbohydrates: 8g
- Dietary Fiber: 5g
- Sugars: 2g
- Fat: 18g
- Sodium: 390mg

Roasted almonds offer a delightful crunch and rich flavor, making them an irresistible treat. Whether paired with a cup of tea or enjoyed alone, these "Delicious Roasted Almonds and Large Pieces" add sophistication and health benefits to your brunch. Indulge without guilt and savor every bite!

Recipe 36: Peanut Butter and Oatmeal Energy Balls

When the morning calls for a boost of energy and flavor, "Peanut Butter and Oatmeal Energy Balls" come to the rescue. These bite-sized treats blend the richness of peanut butter with the wholesomeness of oatmeal, offering a delightful start to your day.

Servings: 10 balls

Prepping Time: 10 minutes

Cook Time: 0 minutes (no-bake)

Difficulty: Easy

Ingredients:

- ✓ 1 cup old-fashioned oats
- ✓ 1/2 cup creamy peanut butter
- ✓ 1/3 cup honey or maple syrup
- ✓ 1/2 cup ground flaxseed

- ✓ 1 tsp vanilla extract
- ✓ 1/2 cup chocolate chips (optional)
- ✓ A pinch of salt

Step-by-Step Preparation:

1. Combine oats, peanut butter, honey, flaxseed, and vanilla extract in a large mixing bowl.
2. Mix well until ingredients are thoroughly combined.
3. Fold in chocolate chips if using.
4. Shape the mixture into balls using your hands.
5. Place on a parchment-lined tray and refrigerate for at least 1 hour before serving.

Nutritional Facts: (Per serving)

- ➢ Calories: 180
- ➢ Protein: 6g
- ➢ Carbohydrates: 20g
- ➢ Dietary Fiber: 3g
- ➢ Sugars: 12g
- ➢ Fat: 10g
- ➢ Sodium: 60mg

With a harmonious blend of textures and flavors, these "Peanut Butter and Oatmeal Energy Balls" are the perfect solution for mid-morning cravings. Nutritious and satisfying, they effortlessly bridge the gap between breakfast and lunch, ensuring your energy levels remain high and your taste buds are delighted.

Recipe 37: Payes With Cinnamon

"Payes with Cinnamon" transports you to a world of aromatic spices and comforting flavors. This traditional rice pudding, with a hint of cinnamon, promises a delightful culinary journey, making it an exceptional addition to any brunch spread.

Servings: 4

Prepping Time: 10 minutes

Cook Time: 45 minutes

Difficulty: Moderate

Ingredients:

- 1 cup Basmati rice
- 5 cups whole milk
- 3/4 cup sugar
- 1 tsp cinnamon powder & A pinch of salt
- 1/4 cup chopped nuts (optional for garnishing)

Step-by-Step Preparation:

1. Wash the rice thoroughly and soak for 30 minutes.
2. In a heavy-bottomed pot, boil the milk.
3. Add the soaked rice to boiling milk and reduce the heat to medium.
4. Cook, stirring occasionally, until the rice is soft and the milk has thickened.
5. Add sugar and mix well.
6. Stir in cinnamon powder and cook for another 5 minutes.
7. Garnish with nuts, if desired, and serve warm.

Nutritional Facts: (Per serving)

- Calories: 310
- Protein: 8g
- Carbohydrates: 58g
- Dietary Fiber: 1g
- Sugars: 39g
- Fat: 6g
- Sodium: 85mg

"Payes with Cinnamon" offers a delicious treat and a nostalgic experience reminiscent of warm family gatherings and festive occasions. This creamy and aromatic rice pudding is a delightful combination of texture and taste that lingers long after the last spoonful.

Recipe 38: Brown Creamy Cocktail Glass

"Brown Creamy Cocktail Glass" is an indulgent drink that merges brunch's luxury with a cocktail's elegance. This drink sets the tone for a sumptuous brunch experience.

Servings: 2

Prepping Time: 5 minutes

Cook Time: No cook time

Difficulty: Easy

Ingredients:

- ✓ 2 oz chocolate liqueur
- ✓ 1 oz coffee liqueur
- ✓ 2 oz heavy cream
- ✓ Crushed ice
- ✓ Cocoa powder for garnish
- ✓ Whipped cream (optional topping)

Step-by-Step Preparation:

1. Fill a cocktail shaker with crushed ice.
2. Pour in the chocolate liqueur, coffee liqueur, and heavy cream.
3. Shake vigorously until well-chilled.
4. Strain the mixture into two cocktail glasses.
5. Optionally, top with whipped cream.
6. Lightly dust with cocoa powder as garnish before serving.

Nutritional Facts: (Per serving)

- Calories: 250
- Protein: 1g
- Carbohydrates: 20g
- Dietary Fiber: 0.5g
- Sugars: 19g
- Fat: 8g
- Sodium: 25mg

The "Brown Creamy Cocktail Glass" is more than just a drink; it's a decadent experience in a glass. Perfect for those laid-back brunch sessions, this cocktail is a delightful blend of flavors to ensure your brunch is remembered long after the last sip.

Recipe 39: Blueberry Squares with Crunchy Topping

When the sweetness of blueberries meets a crispy, buttery topping, you get "Blueberry Squares with Crunchy Topping." These delightful treats offer a fruity flavor, making them an instant hit for any brunch occasion.

Servings: 12

Prepping Time: 15 minutes

Cook Time: 35 minutes

Difficulty: Medium

Ingredients:

- 2 cups fresh blueberries
- 1 cup all-purpose flour & 1/2 cup granulated sugar
- 1/4 cup unsalted butter, softened & 1/4 cup brown sugar
- 1/2 tsp baking powder & 1/4 tsp salt
- 1 large egg & 1 tsp vanilla extract

For the Crunchy Topping:

- ✓ 1/2 cup rolled oats
- ✓ 1/3 cup brown sugar
- ✓ 1/4 cup all-purpose flour
- ✓ 3 tbsp unsalted butter, melted

Step-by-Step Preparation:

1. Preheat the oven to 350°F (175°C) and grease an 8x8-inch baking pan.
2. Combine flour, granulated sugar, baking powder, and salt in a mixing bowl.
3. Mix in the softened butter, egg, and vanilla until smooth.
4. Spread the batter in the prepared pan and top with blueberries.
5. Mix the ingredients for the crunchy topping in a separate bowl until crumbly.
6. Sprinkle the topping over the blueberries.
7. Bake for 35 minutes or until a toothpick comes out clean.
8. Allow to cool before cutting into squares.

Nutritional Facts: (Per serving)

- ➢ Calories: 190
- ➢ Protein: 2g
- ➢ Carbohydrates: 32g
- ➢ Dietary Fiber: 1g
- ➢ Sugars: 20g
- ➢ Fat: 6g
- ➢ Sodium: 55mg

"Blueberry Squares with Crunchy Topping" meld the softness of cake with the texture of crumble, creating a harmonious bite perfect for brunch. This delightful dish is a testament to how simple ingredients produce memorable flavors.

Recipe 40: Chocolate Pomegranate Banana Peanut Butter Shake

Reimagine your regular shakes with the "Healthy Chocolate Pomegranate Banana Peanut Butter Shake." This concoction blends rich chocolate, tangy pomegranate, creamy banana, and savory peanut butter for a delightful brunch sipper.

Servings: 2

Prepping Time: 10 minutes

Cook Time: 0 minutes

Difficulty: Easy

Ingredients:

- ✓ 1 ripe banana
- ✓ 1/4 cup pomegranate seeds
- ✓ 1 tbsp unsweetened cocoa powder
- ✓ 2 tbsp peanut butter

- ✓ 1 cup almond milk (or any milk of choice)
- ✓ 1 tsp honey (optional)
- ✓ A pinch of salt
- ✓ Ice cubes

Step-by-Step Preparation:

1. Add the ripe banana, pomegranate seeds, and ice cubes in a blender.
2. Next, add the desired cocoa powder, peanut butter, and honey.
3. Pour in the almond milk.
4. Blend until smooth and creamy.
5. Taste and adjust sweetness or thickness if needed.
6. Serve immediately in chilled glasses.

Nutritional Facts: (Per serving)

- ➢ Calories: 230
- ➢ Protein: 6g
- ➢ Carbohydrates: 32g
- ➢ Dietary Fiber: 4g
- ➢ Sugars: 18g
- ➢ Fat: 10g
- ➢ Sodium: 90mg

The "Healthy Chocolate Pomegranate Banana Peanut Butter Shake" perfectly balances flavors and health benefits. This shake promises to be a crowd-pleaser, ideal for brunch or any time you crave a sweet, refreshing treat.

Chapter 05: Dinner Delights

Recipe 41: Minced Beef Bolognese Sauce Topped

Dive into rich flavors with the "Minced Beef Bolognese Sauce Topped" dish. This classic Italian staple, boasting a hearty meat sauce, transforms pasta or lasagna into a memorable meal suitable for any dinner occasion.

Servings: 4

Prepping Time: 15 minutes

Cook Time: 1 hour 30 minutes

Difficulty: Medium

Ingredients:

- ✓ 500g minced beef & 1 large onion, finely chopped
- ✓ 2 cloves garlic, minced & 1 carrot, diced
- ✓ 1 celery stalk, diced & 400g canned tomatoes

- ✓ 2 tbsp tomato paste
- ✓ 1/2 cup red wine (optional)
- ✓ 1 tsp dried oregano
- ✓ Salt and pepper to taste
- ✓ 2 tbsp olive oil & Fresh basil leaves for garnish

Step-by-Step Preparation:

1. Heat olive oil in a large pan and sauté onions until translucent.
2. Add garlic, carrots, and celery, cooking until softened.
3. Add the minced beef, breaking it apart, and cook until browned.
4. Stir in the tomato paste, canned tomatoes, and wine (if using).
5. Season with oregano, salt, and pepper.
6. Let it simmer on low heat for about 1-1.5 hours, stirring occasionally.
7. Once thickened, garnish with fresh basil before serving.

Nutritional Facts: (Per serving)

- ➢ Calories: 340
- ➢ Protein: 25g
- ➢ Carbohydrates: 12g
- ➢ Dietary Fiber: 3g
- ➢ Sugars: 6g
- ➢ Fat: 20g
- ➢ Sodium: 420mg

End your day on a high note with the "Minced Beef Bolognese Sauce Topped." Its deep flavors and rich texture make it a dinner favorite. Serve atop your choice of pasta or layered in lasagna, and relish the authentic taste of Italy right at home.

Recipe 42: Kale Quinoa Salad with a Grilled Steak

Savor the best of both worlds with the "Kale Quinoa Salad with a Grilled Steak." This hearty ensemble combines fresh greens and protein-packed grains with the juiciness of grilled steak. Perfect for those who want to maintain taste and health.

Servings: 4

Prepping Time: 20 minutes

Cook Time: 15 minutes

Difficulty: Medium

Ingredients:

- ✓ 4 steak cuts of your choice
- ✓ 2 cups of kale, chopped and de-stemmed
- ✓ 1 cup of cooked quinoa
- ✓ 1 red bell pepper, thinly sliced

- ✓ 1/4 cup feta cheese, crumbled
- ✓ 2 tbsp olive oil
- ✓ 1 tbsp balsamic vinegar
- ✓ Salt and pepper to taste
- ✓ 2 cloves garlic, minced

Step-by-Step Preparation:

1. Preheat the grill to medium-high heat.
2. Season steaks with salt, pepper, and garlic.
3. Grill steaks to the desired doneness, then let them rest.
4. In a large bowl, mix kale, quinoa, and bell pepper.
5. Whisk together olive oil and balsamic vinegar, and drizzle over the salad.
6. Toss the salad top with crumbled feta.
7. Serve salad alongside the grilled steak.

Nutritional Facts: (Per serving)

- ➢ Calories: 450
- ➢ Protein: 40g
- ➢ Carbohydrates: 25g
- ➢ Dietary Fiber: 5g
- ➢ Sugars: 3g
- ➢ Fat: 20g
- ➢ Sodium: 320mg

Elevate your dinner experience with the "Kale Quinoa Salad with a Grilled Steak." This dish nourishes your body and satiates the soul, giving a modern twist to the traditional steak dinner. Embrace a plate full of vibrant colors, textures, and delectable flavors tonight!

Recipe 43: Vegetarian Homemade Pie Quiche with Tomatoes

Whisk your senses away with the "Vegetarian Homemade Pie, Quiche with Tomatoes." This savory masterpiece marries a flaky crust with a lush filling topped with juicy tomatoes, offering an indulgent experience without the meat. Perfect for cozy dinners and gatherings alike.

Servings: 6

Prepping Time: 25 minutes

Cook Time: 35 minutes

Difficulty: Medium

Ingredients:

- 1 prepared pie crust
- 4 large eggs
- 1 cup heavy cream
- 1 cup cheddar cheese, grated

- ✓ 1/2 cup parmesan cheese, grated
- ✓ 2 large tomatoes, thinly sliced
- ✓ 1/4 cup fresh basil, chopped
- ✓ 1/2 teaspoon salt
- ✓ 1/4 teaspoon black pepper
- ✓ 1/2 teaspoon dried oregano

Step-by-Step Preparation:

1. Preheat the oven to 375°F (190°C).
2. Place the pie crust in a pie dish and set aside.
3. Whisk together eggs, heavy cream, salt, pepper, and oregano in a bowl.
4. Stir in cheddar and parmesan cheese.
5. Pour the mixture into the pie crust.
6. Arrange tomato slices on top and sprinkle with basil.
7. Bake for 35 minutes or until set and golden brown.

Nutritional Facts: (Per serving)

- ➢ Calories: 320
- ➢ Protein: 12g
- ➢ Carbohydrates: 18g
- ➢ Dietary Fiber: 1g
- ➢ Sugars: 2g
- ➢ Fat: 22g
- ➢ Sodium: 420mg

The "Vegetarian Homemade Pie, Quiche with Tomatoes" is a culinary journey into comfort. It's not just a pie but a symphony of flavors, capturing the essence of a wholesome, meat-free dinner. Share the warmth, the aroma, and the delight with loved ones tonight!

Recipe 44: Chicken Breasts Cooked on a Summer BBQ

Indulge in the symphony of smoky flavors with Chicken Breasts Cooked on a Summer BBQ. These tender, juicy cuts, infused with the essence of glowing embers, will transport you straight to summertime festivities, even from the heart of your kitchen.

Servings: 4

Prepping Time: 15 minutes (plus margination time)

Cook Time: 20 minutes

Difficulty: Easy

Ingredients:

- 4 boneless, skinless chicken breasts
- 1/4 cup olive oil
- 3 tablespoons lemon juice
- 2 cloves garlic, minced
- 1 tablespoon fresh rosemary, chopped

- ✓ Salt and pepper, to taste
- ✓ 1 teaspoon smoked paprika

Step-by-Step Preparation:

1. Mix olive oil, lemon juice, garlic, rosemary, salt, pepper, and paprika in a bowl.
2. Coat chicken breasts in the mixture and marinate for at least 2 hours.
3. Preheat the BBQ grill to medium-high heat.
4. Grill chicken breasts on each side for 8-10 minutes until fully cooked and slightly charred.
5. Let rest for 5 minutes before serving.

Nutritional Facts: (Per serving)

- ➢ Calories: 270
- ➢ Protein: 31g
- ➢ Carbohydrates: 2g
- ➢ Dietary Fiber: 0.5g
- ➢ Sugars: 0.8g
- ➢ Fat: 15g
- ➢ Sodium: 120mg

Revel in the nostalgic charm of summer nights with "Chicken Breasts Cooked on a Summer BBQ." This dish epitomizes the spirit of outdoor cookouts, promising each bite to be an echo of laughter, warm breezes, and unforgettable memories. Share, savor, and celebrate!

Recipe 45: Vegan Strudel with Lentils

Dive into a world of rich, savory flavors with the "Vegan Strudel with Lentils." This delightful twist on a classic offers a hearty lentil filling wrapped in a crispy, golden pastry, making every bite an unforgettable fusion of taste and texture.

Servings: 6

Prepping Time: 20 minutes

Cook Time: 35 minutes

Difficulty: Moderate

Ingredients:

- 1 roll of vegan puff pastry
- 2 cups cooked lentils
- 1 medium onion, finely chopped
- 2 cloves garlic, minced
- 1 carrot, diced
- 1 celery stalk, diced

- ✓ 2 tablespoons olive oil
- ✓ 1 teaspoon thyme
- ✓ Salt and pepper, to taste

Step-by-Step Preparation:

1. Preheat oven to 375°F (190°C).
2. In a pan, sauté onion, garlic, carrot, and celery in olive oil until softened.
3. Add lentils, thyme, salt, and pepper; cook for 5 minutes.
4. Roll out the puff pastry and spread the lentil mixture down the center.
5. Fold the pastry over the filling and seal the edges.
6. Place on a baking sheet and bake for 25-30 minutes until golden brown.

Nutritional Facts. (Per serving)

- ➢ Calories: 290
- ➢ Protein: 10g
- ➢ Carbohydrates: 38g
- ➢ Dietary Fiber: 8g
- ➢ Sugars: 3g
- ➢ Fat: 12g
- ➢ Sodium: 180mg

The "Vegan Strudel with Lentils" is more than just a dish; it's a culinary experience. A perfect combination of health and indulgence, this strudel promises a delightful end to any dinner, ensuring satisfied smiles all around the table.

Recipe 46: Fish and Tamarind-Based Soup

Immerse yourself in the tangy and savory blend of the "Fish and Tamarind-Based Soup." A cherished culinary treasure, this soup tantalizes the palate with its rich broth, melding the freshness of fish with the distinctive sourness of tamarind.

Servings: 4

Prepping Time: 15 minutes

Cook Time: 30 minutes

Difficulty: Easy

Ingredients:

- ✓ 2 fillets of white fish, cut into chunks
- ✓ 1/4 cup tamarind paste
- ✓ 4 cups of water
- ✓ 1 tomato, diced
- ✓ 1 onion, thinly sliced

- ✓ 2 cloves garlic, minced
- ✓ 2 green chilies, sliced
- ✓ 2 tablespoons fish sauce
- ✓ 1 tablespoon vegetable oil
- ✓ Fresh cilantro and green onions for garnish

Step-by-Step Preparation:

1. In a pot, heat the oil and sauté onions, garlic, and tomatoes until softened.
2. Pour in water and bring to a boil.
3. Stir in tamarind paste, fish sauce, and green chilies.
4. Add fish chunks and let simmer for 15-20 minutes or until fish is cooked.
5. Adjust seasoning as desired.
6. Garnish with cilantro and green onions before serving.

Nutritional Facts: (Per serving)

- ➤ Calories: 170
- ➤ Protein: 22g
- ➤ Carbohydrates: 12g
- ➤ Dietary Fiber: 1g
- ➤ Sugars: 7g
- ➤ Fat: 3g
- ➤ Sodium: 520mg

The "Fish and Tamarind-Based Soup" offers various flavors in every spoonful. Perfect for a comforting dinner, it warms the heart and soul, bringing joy and a touch of exoticism to your dining experience.

Recipe 47: Baked Salmon Served with Chips

Dive into a delightful dining experience with "Baked Salmon Served with Chips." The union of flaky, seasoned salmon and the crunch of perfectly baked chips promises a perfect balance between gourmet and comfort food.

Servings: 4

Prepping Time: 20 minutes

Cook Time: 25 minutes

Difficulty: Easy

Ingredients:

- ✓ 4 salmon fillets
- ✓ 3 tablespoons olive oil
- ✓ 1 teaspoon salt
- ✓ 1/2 teaspoon black pepper
- ✓ 1 teaspoon garlic powder
- ✓ 4 large potatoes, thinly sliced

- ✓ 2 tablespoons fresh dill, chopped
- ✓ Lemon wedges for serving

Step-by-Step Preparation:

1. Preheat the oven to 400°F (200°C).
2. Toss potato slices in 2 tablespoons of olive oil, salt, and pepper. Arrange on a baking sheet.
3. Place salmon fillets on another baking sheet, drizzle with 1 tablespoon olive oil, and season with salt, pepper, and garlic powder.
4. Bake potatoes and salmon for 20-25 minutes, or until the salmon is flaky and the potatoes are golden.
5. Garnish salmon with fresh dill.
6. Serve with lemon wedges.

Nutritional Facts: (Per serving)

- ➢ Calories: 410
- ➢ Protein: 34g
- ➢ Carbohydrates: 26g
- ➢ Dietary Fiber: 3g
- ➢ Sugars: 1g
- ➢ Fat: 18g
- ➢ Sodium: 620mg

The "Baked Salmon Served with Chips" offers a mouthwatering twist on a classic favorite. This dish is a testament to the magic that unfolds when simplicity meets sophistication.

Recipe 48: Spaghetti Squash with Marinara and Meatballs

Elevate your dinner game with "Spaghetti Squash with Marinara and Meatballs." This wholesome dish reimagines the traditional pasta favorite, offering a low-carb twist without compromising on taste or satisfaction.

Servings: 4

Prepping Time: 20 minutes

Cook Time: 60 minutes

Difficulty: Medium

Ingredients:

- 1 large spaghetti squash, halved and seeds removed
- 1 tablespoon olive oil
- 1 teaspoon salt
- 1/2 teaspoon black pepper
- 2 cups marinara sauce

- ✓ 12 meatballs (beef or turkey)
- ✓ 1/2 cup grated Parmesan cheese
- ✓ Fresh basil for garnish

Step-by-Step Preparation:

1. Preheat the oven to 400°F (200°C).
2. Brush the inner flesh of spaghetti squash with olive oil and sprinkle with salt and pepper.
3. Place the squash, cut side down, on a baking sheet and bake for 40 minutes.
4. In a saucepan, heat the marinara sauce and add meatballs. Simmer for 20 minutes.
5. Use a fork to shred the cooked squash into spaghetti-like strands.
6. Serve squash topped with marinara meatballs, a sprinkle of Parmesan, and garnished with fresh basil.

Nutritional Facts: (Per serving)

- ➢ Calories: 310
- ➢ Protein: 17g
- ➢ Carbohydrates: 38g
- ➢ Dietary Fiber: 7g
- ➢ Sugars: 12g
- ➢ Fat: 12g
- ➢ Sodium: 860mg

The "Spaghetti Squash with Marinara and Meatballs" dish beckons those yearning for a hearty meal with a healthy edge. This delightful dinner blend proves that nutritious choices can burst with flavors that leave you craving more.

Recipe 49: Beef Stew Cooked with Pomegranate and Herbs

Experience traditional and exotic fusion with the "Beef Stew Cooked with Pomegranate and Herbs." The tangy pomegranate and aromatic herbs elevate the humble beef stew to a gourmet experience.

Servings: 4

Prepping Time: 25 minutes

Cook Time: 2 hours 30 minutes

Difficulty: Medium

Ingredients:

- ✓ 500g beef chunks
- ✓ 1 cup pomegranate juice
- ✓ 2 tablespoons pomegranate seeds
- ✓ 1 onion, finely chopped
- ✓ 2 garlic cloves, minced

- ✓ 1 bay leaf
- ✓ 1 teaspoon rosemary, finely chopped
- ✓ 1 teaspoon thyme, finely chopped
- ✓ 2 cups beef broth
- ✓ 1 tablespoon olive oil
- ✓ Salt and pepper to taste

Step-by-Step Preparation:

1. Heat olive oil in a large pot over medium heat. Add onions and garlic, sautéing until translucent.
2. Add beef chunks and brown on all sides.
3. Pour in pomegranate juice, beef broth, and herbs. Season with salt and pepper.
4. Bring to a boil, then reduce to a simmer, covering the pot.
5. Cook for 2 hours or until beef is tender.
6. Garnish with pomegranate seeds before serving.

Nutritional Facts: (Per serving)

- ➢ Calories: 370
- ➢ Protein: 28g
- ➢ Carbohydrates: 18g
- ➢ Dietary Fiber: 2g
- ➢ Sugars: 12g
- ➢ Fat: 20g
- ➢ Sodium: 740mg

The "Beef Stew Cooked with Pomegranate and Herbs" is a dinner masterpiece that marries rich flavors and nutritional goodness. Each bite promises a symphony of taste, ensuring a memorable dining experience.

Recipe 50: Eggplant Chickpeas Peas Vegetarian Vegan Curry

Indulge in the rich and aromatic flavors of the "Eggplant Chickpeas Peas Vegetarian Vegan Curry." This sumptuous dish, brimming with hearty vegetables and a fragrant mix of spices, promises a culinary journey that's both satisfying and wholesome.

Servings: 4

Prepping Time: 20 minutes

Cook Time: 40 minutes

Difficulty: Moderate

Ingredients:

- ✓ 2 medium eggplants, cubed
- ✓ 1 cup chickpeas, soaked and boiled
- ✓ 1 cup green peas & 1 onion, finely chopped
- ✓ 2 tomatoes, pureed & 2 garlic cloves, minced

- ✓ 1-inch ginger, grated
- ✓ 2 green chilies, slit
- ✓ 2 teaspoons curry powder
- ✓ 1 teaspoon turmeric powder
- ✓ 1 teaspoon cumin seeds
- ✓ 2 tablespoons olive oil
- ✓ Salt to taste & Fresh cilantro for garnish

Step-by-Step Preparation:

1. Heat olive oil in a pan. Add cumin seeds and wait till they sizzle.
2. Add onions, garlic, ginger, and green chilies. Sauté until onions turn golden.
3. Stir in the tomato puree, turmeric, and curry powder. Cook until oil separates.
4. Add eggplant, chickpeas, and peas to the pan. Mix well.
5. Cover and let it simmer for 30 minutes or until vegetables are tender.
6. Garnish with fresh cilantro before serving.

Nutritional Facts: (Per serving)

- ➢ Calories: 240
- ➢ Protein: 9g
- ➢ Carbohydrates: 40g
- ➢ Dietary Fiber: 12g
- ➢ Sugars: 10g
- ➢ Fat: 7g
- ➢ Sodium: 240mg

This "Eggplant Chickpeas Peas Vegetarian Vegan Curry" is a flavorful blend of hearty veggies and rich spices. Perfect for those cozy dinner nights, it's a delightful treat that warms the heart and satisfies the soul.

Chapter 06: Midnight Munchies

Recipe 51: Vegan Chocolate Truffles Balls

Are you craving a late-night sweet treat? These "Vegan Chocolate Truffles Balls" offer the perfect bite-sized indulgence. With a velvety center and a rich chocolatey exterior, each ball is a testament to guilt-free pleasure, making midnight munching an absolute delight.

Servings: 12

Prepping Time: 15 minutes

Cook Time: 2 hours (chilling time)

Difficulty: Easy

Ingredients:

- ✓ 1 cup vegan dark chocolate, chopped
- ✓ 1/2 cup coconut milk, full-fat
- ✓ 1 teaspoon vanilla extract

- ✓ A pinch of sea salt
- ✓ Cocoa powder for dusting

Step-by-Step Preparation:

1. Heat coconut milk in a saucepan until it simmers.
2. Pour hot coconut milk over chopped chocolate and let sit for a minute.
3. Stir the mixture until smooth, then add vanilla extract and sea salt.
4. Refrigerate the mixture for about 2 hours or until firm.
5. Once firm, roll into small balls and coat with cocoa powder.

Nutritional Facts: (Per serving)

- ➤ Calories: 110
- ➤ Protein: 1g
- ➤ Carbohydrates: 9g
- ➤ Dietary Fiber: 2g
- ➤ Sugars: 6g
- ➤ Fat: 8g
- ➤ Sodium: 10mg

Indulge your late-night cravings with the "Vegan Chocolate Truffles Balls," a decadent delight perfect for a quick chocolate fix. With their melt-in-the-mouth texture, these truffles promise a luxurious experience with every bite.

Recipe 52: Peanut Butter Sandwich Vegetarian Food

There's nothing quite like the classic comfort of a "Peanut Butter Sandwich" during those midnight hunger pangs. This vegetarian delight is simple yet satisfying, offering a blend of nutty richness and velvety smoothness with every bite.

Servings: 2

Prepping Time: 5 minutes

Cook Time: 0 minutes

Difficulty: Easy

Ingredients:

- ✓ 4 slices of whole wheat bread
- ✓ 4 tablespoons peanut butter (creamy or chunky as preferred)
- ✓ Optional toppings: sliced bananas, honey, or jam

Step-by-Step Preparation:

1. Lay out the slices of bread on a flat surface.
2. Spread a generous layer of peanut butter onto two slices.
3. Add optional toppings if desired.
4. Top with the remaining pieces of bread. Press gently.

Nutritional Facts: (Per serving)

- Calories: 330
- Protein: 12g
- Carbohydrates: 38g
- Dietary Fiber: 6g
- Sugars: 6g
- Fat: 18g
- Sodium: 300mg

The "Peanut Butter Sandwich" is a timeless midnight snack, reminding us that the simplest pleasures are sometimes the best. Whether studying late or enjoying a quiet moment, this sandwich offers a wholesome treat to satisfy those late-night

Recipe 53: Grilled Salmon Trout Fish with Spices Lemon

Are you craving something savory and delightful during the wee hours? This "Grilled Salmon Trout Fish with Spices and Lemon" is a light yet flavorful option for late-night gourmet indulgence. Infused with spices and a zesty lemon touch, it promises a compelling experience.

Servings: 2

Prepping Time: 10 minutes

Cook Time: 15 minutes

Difficulty: Medium

Ingredients:

- 2 salmon trout fillets
- 1 tablespoon olive oil
- 1 teaspoon paprika
- 1/2 teaspoon black pepper
- 1/2 teaspoon sea salt

- ✓ Zest and juice of 1 lemon
- ✓ Fresh dill or parsley for garnish

Step-by-Step Preparation:

1. Preheat the grill to medium-high heat.
2. Drizzle olive oil over the salmon trout fillets.
3. Mix paprika, black pepper, salt, and lemon zest in a small bowl. Rub this mixture over the fillets.
4. Place the seasoned fillets on the grill and cook for 6-7 minutes on each side or until fully cooked.
5. Before serving, drizzle with fresh lemon juice and garnish with dill or parsley.

Nutritional Facts: (Per serving)

- ➢ Calories: 280
- ➢ Protein: 25g
- ➢ Carbohydrates: 2g
- ➢ Dietary Fiber: 0.5g
- ➢ Sugars: 0.5g
- ➢ Fat: 18g
- ➢ Sodium: 590mg

This "Grilled Salmon Trout Fish" dish stands out when midnight cravings demand luxury. The fusion of spices with a hint of lemon ensures every bite is an exquisite blend of taste and texture. Perfect for those who love a little gourmet touch to their late-night treats.

Recipe 54: Fresh Popcorn with Chili Pepper

There's nothing like the comforting sound of popping corn when late-night hunger strikes. It's the perfect blend of warmth and zest, giving a fiery kick to every crunchy bite.

Servings: 4

Prepping Time: 2 minutes

Cook Time: 5 minutes

Difficulty: Easy

Ingredients:

- 1/2 cup popcorn kernels
- 2 tablespoons vegetable oil
- 1 teaspoon chili pepper powder (adjust to taste)
- Salt to taste
- Melted butter (optional)

Step-by-Step Preparation:

1. In a large pot, heat the vegetable oil over medium heat.
2. Once hot, add the popcorn kernels, ensuring an even layer at the bottom.
3. Cover the pot with a lid and let the kernels pop, shaking occasionally.
4. Once the popping slows down, could you remove it from the heat?
5. Sprinkle chili pepper and salt over the popcorn. Drizzle with melted butter if desired. Toss well.

Nutritional Facts: (Per serving)

- Calories: 90
- Protein: 2g
- Carbohydrates: 15g
- Dietary Fiber: 3g
- Sugars: 0g
- Fat: 3g
- Sodium: 290mg

"Fresh Popcorn with Chili Pepper" is a must-try for those craving a spicy twist on a classic snack. It's a midnight munchie that'll warm you up and keep those taste buds dancing, perfect for movie nights or when you need a flavorful pick-me-up.

Recipe 55: Muesli Bar Partially Covered with Dry Fruits and One Bit

When midnight cravings come calling, satiate them with a nutritious yet delightful treat. Dive into the layers of a Muesli Bar adorned with dry fruits, revealing a bite of wholesomeness. It's the perfect balance of sweet, crunchy, and a tad bit chewy.

Servings: 8 bars

Prepping Time: 15 minutes

Cook Time: 25 minutes

Difficulty: Moderate

Ingredients:

- 2 cups rolled oats
- 1 cup mixed dry fruits (raisins, apricots, and cranberries)
- 1/2 cup honey or maple syrup
- 1/4 cup unsalted butter, melted

- ✓ 1/2 teaspoon vanilla extract
- ✓ A pinch of salt

Step-by-Step Preparation:

1. Preheat the oven to 350°F (175°C) and line an 8-inch square baking pan with parchment paper.
2. Combine oats, half of the dry fruits, honey, melted butter, vanilla, and salt in a large mixing bowl. Mix until well combined.
3. Press the mixture firmly into the prepared baking pan.
4. Sprinkle the remaining dry fruits, pressing them slightly into the mixture.
5. Bake for 20-25 minutes until the edges are golden.
6. Allow to cool completely before cutting into bars.

Nutritional Facts: (Per serving)

- ➢ Calories: 220
- ➢ Protein: 4g
- ➢ Carbohydrates: 38g
- ➢ Dietary Fiber: 3g
- ➢ Sugars: 24g
- ➢ Fat: 7g
- ➢ Sodium: 20mg

These Muesli Bars, studded with dry fruits and presenting a delightful bite, are the quintessential midnight snack. They satisfy your sweet tooth and offer a burst of energy, making them perfect for late-night study sessions or binge-watching your favorite shows.

Recipe 56: Slice of Vegan Cheesecake Made with Plant Protein Powder

When midnight indulgence is paired with health-consciousness, you get this Slice of Vegan Cheesecake. Rich in flavor and made with plant protein powder, this cheesecake promises a guilt-free decadence, sure to satisfy your nocturnal sweet cravings.

Servings: 8 slices

Prepping Time: 20 minutes

Cook Time: 40 minutes

Difficulty: Intermediate

Ingredients:

- ✓ 1 1/2 cups raw cashews, soaked overnight
- ✓ 1/4 cup plant protein powder
- ✓ 1/2 cup coconut milk
- ✓ 1/3 cup maple syrup or agave nectar

- ✓ 2 tsp vanilla extract
- ✓ 1/4 cup coconut oil, melted
- ✓ 1 pre-made vegan graham cracker crust
- ✓ A pinch of salt

Step-by-Step Preparation:

1. Preheat oven to 325°F (163°C).
2. Combine soaked cashews, plant protein powder, coconut milk, maple syrup, vanilla extract, and salt in a blender. Blend until smooth.
3. Slowly add in melted coconut oil while the blender is running.
4. Pour the mixture over the pre-made crust, smoothing the top with a spatula.
5. Bake for 40 minutes or until set.
6. Allow to cool, then refrigerate for at least 4 hours before serving.

Nutritional Facts: (Per serving)

- ➢ Calories: 280
- ➢ Protein: 8g
- ➢ Carbohydrates: 25g
- ➢ Dietary Fiber: 1g
- ➢ Sugars: 18g
- ➢ Fat: 18g
- ➢ Sodium: 90mg

Give in to your midnight dessert desires with this Vegan Cheesecake slice. It delivers a burst of creamy delight, and the added plant protein also provides a nutritional edge. Perfect for fitness enthusiasts with a sweet tooth or anyone looking for a guilt-free treat!

Recipe 57: Freshly Baked Blueberry Muffins

Midnight cravings can be a delightful experience, especially with these Freshly Baked Blueberry Muffins. These muffins encapsulate the sweet tanginess of blueberries within a soft, moist crumb, making them a perfect late-night snack or early-morning treat.

Servings: 12 muffins

Prepping Time: 15 minutes

Cook Time: 25 minutes

Difficulty: Easy

Ingredients:

- 2 cups all-purpose flour
- 1 1/2 tsp baking powder
- 1/2 tsp baking soda
- 1/2 cup unsalted butter, softened
- 1 cup granulated sugar

- ✓ 2 large eggs
- ✓ 2 tsp vanilla extract
- ✓ 1/2 cup milk
- ✓ 1 1/2 cups fresh blueberries

Step-by-Step Preparation:

1. Preheat oven to 375°F (190°C) and line a muffin tin with paper liners.
2. In a bowl, mix flour, baking powder, and baking soda.
3. In another bowl, cream butter and sugar until light and fluffy.
4. Add eggs one at a time, followed by vanilla.
5. Gradually mix in dry ingredients, alternating with milk.
6. Gently fold in blueberries.
7. Divide batter among muffin cups.
8. Bake for 25 minutes or until a toothpick comes out clean.

Nutritional Facts: (Per serving)

- ➢ Calories: 210
- ➢ Protein: 3g
- ➢ Carbohydrates: 32g
- ➢ Dietary Fiber: 1g
- ➢ Sugars: 18g
- ➢ Fat: 8g
- ➢ Sodium: 90mg

Why wait for breakfast when you can satisfy your cravings with these Freshly Baked Blueberry Muffins right now? Dive into the burst of fresh blueberries enveloped in a delicate crumb, making your midnight a delightful and indulgent journey.

Recipe 58: Cake with Chocolate and Sea Salt

As the clock strikes midnight, let your taste buds dance to the symphony of Cake with Chocolate and Sea Salt. This indulgent treat marries the sweetness of chocolate with the contrasting kick of sea salt for an unforgettable dessert rendezvous.

Servings: 8

Prepping Time: 20 minutes

Cook Time: 35 minutes

Difficulty: Intermediate

Ingredients:

- ✓ 1 3/4 cups all-purpose flour
- ✓ 1 1/2 tsp baking powder
- ✓ 1/2 cup unsweetened cocoa powder
- ✓ 1 cup granulated sugar
- ✓ 1/2 cup unsalted butter, melted

- ✓ 2 large eggs
- ✓ 1 tsp vanilla extract
- ✓ 1 1/4 cups milk
- ✓ 1/2 tsp flaky sea salt

Step-by-Step Preparation:

1. Preheat oven to 350°F (175°C) and grease a 9-inch cake pan.
2. In a bowl, whisk flour, baking powder, and cocoa.
3. Combine melted butter, sugar, eggs, and vanilla in another bowl.
4. Gradually mix in the dry ingredients, followed by milk.
5. Pour the batter into the prepared pan.
6. Sprinkle sea salt evenly over the top.
7. Bake for 35 minutes or until a toothpick comes out mostly clean.

Nutritional Facts: (Per serving)

- ➢ Calories: 290
- ➢ Protein: 5g
- ➢ Carbohydrates: 42g
- ➢ Dietary Fiber: 2g
- ➢ Sugars: 24g
- ➢ Fat: 12g
- ➢ Sodium: 170mg

Elevate your late-night dessert experience with the Cake with Chocolate and Sea Salt. Dive into the velvety chocolate layers accentuated with a hint of sea salt, making each bite a perfect balance of sweet and savory. Midnight has never tasted this grand!

Recipe 59: A Nutty Milk Chocolate Coated Brownies

Indulge in the rich decadence of A Nutty Milk Chocolate Coated Brownies. These brownies offer a luxurious blend of velvety chocolate and crunchy nuts, perfect for those midnight cravings, promising pure dessert delight.

Servings: 12

Prepping Time: 20 minutes

Cook Time: 25 minutes

Difficulty: Intermediate

Ingredients:

- 1 cup all-purpose flour
- 1/2 cup unsweetened cocoa powder
- 1/4 tsp salt
- 1/2 cup unsalted butter, melted
- 1 cup granulated sugar

- ✓ 2 large eggs
- ✓ 1 tsp vanilla extract
- ✓ 1/2 cup chopped mixed nuts (e.g., walnuts, pecans)
- ✓ 1 cup milk chocolate chips

Step-by-Step Preparation:

1. Preheat oven to 350°F (175°C) and grease an 8-inch square baking pan.
2. Mix flour, cocoa, and salt in a bowl.
3. Beat melted butter, sugar, eggs, and vanilla in a separate bowl.
4. Combine wet and dry ingredients and fold in nuts.
5. Spread the batter in the pan.
6. Bake for 25 minutes.
7. Melt milk chocolate chips and spread over baked brownies. Allow to set.

Nutritional Facts: (Per serving)

- ➢ Calories: 310
- ➢ Protein: 5g
- ➢ Carbohydrates: 38g
- ➢ Dietary Fiber: 2g
- ➢ Sugars: 25g
- ➢ Fat: 18g
- ➢ Sodium: 60mg

Treat yourself to the sublime fusion of nutty crunch and creamy chocolate with Nutty Milk Chocolate Coated Brownies. It's the dreamy midnight delight you never knew you needed until now!

Recipe 60: Pancakes

When midnight hunger strikes, nothing satisfies like a stack of fluffy pancakes. Warm, buttery, and drizzled with syrup, they're the ultimate comfort food to indulge in, no matter the hour.

Servings: 4

Prepping Time: 10 minutes

Cook Time: 15 minutes

Difficulty: Easy

Ingredients:

- 1 cup all-purpose flour
- 2 tbsp granulated sugar
- 1 tsp baking powder
- 1/2 tsp baking soda
- 1/4 tsp salt
- 3/4 cup buttermilk

- ✓ 1 large egg
- ✓ 2 tbsp unsalted butter, melted
- ✓ Maple syrup and additional butter for serving

Step-by-Step Preparation:

1. Whisk together flour, sugar, baking powder, baking soda, and salt in a bowl.
2. In another bowl, combine buttermilk, egg, and melted butter.
3. Mix wet ingredients into the dry until just combined.
4. Heat a non-stick skillet over medium heat.
5. Pour 1/4 cup batter for each pancake.
6. Cook until bubbles form, flip, and cook until golden brown.
7. Serve with butter and maple syrup.

Nutritional Facts: (Per serving)

- ➤ Calories: 230
- ➤ Protein: 6g
- ➤ Carbohydrates: 35g
- ➤ Dietary Fiber: 1g
- ➤ Sugars: 10g
- ➤ Fat: 7g
- ➤ Sodium: 400mg

Whether it's a midnight craving or a breakfast treat, these pancakes always hit the spot. Warm, fluffy, and oh-so-delicious, you'll reach for just one more.

Chapter 07: Seafood Specials

Recipe 61: Seared Portuguese Scallops in a White Wine Lemon Garlic Sauce

For seafood lovers, a few dishes, like Seared Portuguese Scallops, tantalize the taste buds. This recipe, drizzled in a delicate white wine lemon garlic sauce, brings a touch of the Iberian coast to your plate, making every bite an unforgettable experience.

Servings: 4

Prepping Time: 15 minutes

Cook Time: 10 minutes

Difficulty: Medium

Ingredients:

- ✓ 12 large scallops, patted dry
- ✓ 2 tbsp olive oil

- ✓ 1/4 cup white wine
- ✓ Juice of 1 lemon
- ✓ 3 garlic cloves, minced
- ✓ 2 tbsp fresh parsley, chopped
- ✓ Salt and pepper to taste

Step-by-Step Preparation:

1. Heat olive oil in a pan over medium-high heat.
2. Season scallops with salt and pepper and sear for 1-2 minutes on each side until golden.
3. Remove scallops and set aside.
4. In the same pan, add minced garlic and sauté until fragrant.
5. Deglaze the pan with white wine and lemon juice.
6. Return the scallops to the pan and sprinkle with fresh parsley.
7. Serve immediately.

Nutritional Facts: (Per serving)

- ➢ Calories: 150
- ➢ Protein: 14g
- ➢ Carbohydrates: 3g
- ➢ Dietary Fiber: 0g
- ➢ Sugars: 0.5g
- ➢ Fat: 7g
- ➢ Sodium: 200mg

Dive into a world of flavors with these Portuguese Scallops. The perfect balance of tangy, savory, and seared perfection, this dish will transport your senses straight to the beaches of Portugal. A true seafood special for any occasion!

Recipe 62: Cilantro-Lime Grilled Tuna with Avocado Cucumber Salsa

Indulge in a taste of the tropics with Cilantro-Lime Grilled Tuna, complemented by an Avocado Cucumber Salsa. This dish pairs the rich flavors of fresh tuna with a zesty, refreshing salsa, delivering a delightful fusion of textures and tastes.

Servings: 4

Prepping Time: 20 minutes

Cook Time: 8 minutes

Difficulty: Medium

Ingredients:

- 4 tuna steaks (6 oz each)
- 2 tbsp olive oil
- Juice of 2 limes
- 1/4 cup fresh cilantro, chopped

- ✓ 1 avocado, diced
- ✓ 1 cucumber, diced
- ✓ 1 small red onion, finely chopped
- ✓ 1 jalapeño, seeded and minced
- ✓ Salt and pepper to taste

Step-by-Step Preparation:

1. Whisk together olive oil, lime juice, half of the cilantro, salt, and pepper in a bowl.
2. Marinate tuna steaks in the mixture for 15 minutes.
3. While marinating tuna, combine avocado, cucumber, red onion, jalapeño, remaining cilantro, salt, and pepper to make the salsa
4. Grill tuna steaks on high heat for 3-4 minutes on each side or to desired doneness.
5. Serve grilled tuna topped with avocado cucumber salsa.

Nutritional Facts: (Per serving)

- ➢ Calories: 340
- ➢ Protein: 40g
- ➢ Carbohydrates: 12g
- ➢ Dietary Fiber: 7g
- ➢ Sugars: 3g
- ➢ Fat: 16g
- ➢ Sodium: 65mg

With every bite of this Cilantro-Lime Grilled Tuna, be transported to a seaside escape. The accompanying Avocado Cucumber Salsa adds a refreshing crunch and amplifies the dish's vibrancy, making it a seafood specialty to remember.

Recipe 63: A Delicious Salmon Burger with Lettuce

Experience the exquisite taste of the ocean with a twist in this Delicious Salmon Burger with Lettuce. This burger is a delightful departure from the ordinary, offering a refreshing seafood flavor in every bite.

Servings: 4

Prepping Time: 15 minutes

Cook Time: 10 minutes

Difficulty: Medium

Ingredients:

- ✓ 1 lb. fresh salmon fillet, skin removed
- ✓ 2 tbsp breadcrumbs
- ✓ 1 egg, lightly beaten
- ✓ 2 green onions, chopped
- ✓ 1 tbsp Dijon mustard

- ✓ 1 tbsp lemon juice
- ✓ Salt and pepper to taste
- ✓ 4 whole grain buns
- ✓ 4 lettuce leaves
- ✓ Optional toppings: sliced tomato, onion, and tartar sauce

Step-by-Step Preparation:

1. In a food processor, pulse salmon until finely chopped but not pasty.
2. Transfer to a bowl, and mix with breadcrumbs, egg, green onions, mustard, lemon juice, salt, and pepper.
3. Shape into four patties.
4. Grill or pan-fry over medium heat for 4-5 minutes on each side.
5. Serve on buns with a lettuce leaf and any additional desired toppings.

Nutritional Facts: (Per serving)

- ➢ Calories: 280
- ➢ Protein: 25g
- ➢ Carbohydrates: 23g
- ➢ Dietary Fiber: 3g
- ➢ Sugars: 4g
- ➢ Fat: 8g
- ➢ Sodium: 310mg

Transform your burger night with the Delicious Salmon Burger with Lettuce. With the perfect blend of textures and rich seafood flavor, this burger will become a staple in your seafood specials rotation. Enjoy every sumptuous bite!

Recipe 64: Zucchini Salad with Prawns Flatley on a Marble Countertop

Dive into a vibrant, fresh culinary experience with the Zucchini Salad and succulent prawns. This dish captures the essence of gourmet seafood, blending crisp vegetables with juicy prawns for an unbeatable combination.

Servings: 4

Prepping Time: 20 minutes

Cook Time: 10 minutes

Difficulty: Easy

Ingredients:

- ✓ 4 medium zucchinis, spiralized or thinly sliced
- ✓ 16 large prawns, peeled and deveined
- ✓ 2 tbsp olive oil
- ✓ 1 lemon, zested and juiced
- ✓ 2 cloves garlic, minced

- ✓ Salt and pepper to taste
- ✓ 1/4 cup chopped fresh parsley
- ✓ 1/4 cup grated Parmesan cheese (optional)

Step-by-Step Preparation:

1. Combine spiralized zucchini, lemon zest, and juice in a large bowl.
2. In a pan over medium heat, warm olive oil. Add garlic and sauté until fragrant.
3. Add prawns and cook until pink and opaque, about 4 minutes on each side.
4. Toss the cooked prawns into the zucchini mixture.
5. Season with salt and pepper, and mix in parsley.
6. If desired, sprinkle with Parmesan before serving.

Nutritional Facts: (Per serving)

- ➢ Calories: 180
- ➢ Protein: 15g
- ➢ Carbohydrates: 10g
- ➢ Dietary Fiber: 2g
- ➢ Sugars: 1g
- ➢ Fat: 9g
- ➢ Sodium: 250mg

The Zucchini Salad with Prawns, presented flatly on a marble surface, is a feast for the eyes and an irresistible treat for the taste buds. Fresh, light, and flavorful, it epitomizes seafood elegance. Enjoy this exquisite Seafood Special at any time of the year.

Recipe 65: Steamed Cod with Olive Tapenade

Discover the refined taste of the ocean with the Steamed Cod with Olive Tapenade. Delicately steamed to perfection, the flaky cod pairs harmoniously with the rich, salty flavors of the tapenade. It's an elegant dance of simple ingredients meeting gourmet preparation.

Servings: 4

Prepping Time: 15 minutes

Cook Time: 20 minutes

Difficulty: Medium

Ingredients:

- 4 cod fillets
- 1 cup black olives, pitted
- 2 cloves garlic, minced
- 2 tbsp capers, drained
- 3 tbsp olive oil

- ✓ 1 lemon, zested and juiced
- ✓ Salt and pepper to taste
- ✓ Fresh parsley for garnish

Step-by-Step Preparation:

1. Combine olives, garlic, capers, 2 tbsp olive oil, lemon zest, and juice in a blender to create the tapenade. Blend until smooth.
2. Season the cod fillets with salt and pepper.
3. Steam the cod for about 10-12 minutes or until the fish easily flakes in a steamer or a pot with a steamer insert.
4. Drizzle the remaining olive oil over the steamed cod.
5. Serve the cod hot with a generous spoonful of olive tapenade and garnish with parsley.

Nutritional Facts: (Per serving)

- ➢ Calories: 230
- ➢ Protein: 28g
- ➢ Carbohydrates: 4g
- ➢ Dietary Fiber: 1g
- ➢ Sugars: 1g
- ➢ Fat: 12g
- ➢ Sodium: 450mg

Steamed Cod with Olive Tapenade offers a symphony of Mediterranean flavors in each bite. The salty depth of the tapenade complements the mild, flaky cod, making this Seafood Special a must-try for anyone keen on exploring the rich tapestry of oceanic delights

Recipe 66: Pumpkin Soup with Quinoa and Spinach

Dive into a comforting bowl of Pumpkin Soup with Quinoa and Spinach. This seafood-infused twist on a classic soup showcases the creamy pumpkin base, elevated with hearty quinoa, fresh spinach, and tender seafood morsels. It's a delightful ocean-meets-garden culinary experience.

Servings: 4

Prepping Time: 20 minutes

Cook Time: 35 minutes

Difficulty: Medium

Ingredients:

- ✓ 1 small pumpkin, peeled and cubed
- ✓ 1 cup quinoa, rinsed and drained
- ✓ 3 cups fresh spinach, chopped & 1 onion, diced
- ✓ 2 cloves garlic, minced

- ✓ 1-liter vegetable or fish stock
- ✓ 1 cup mixed seafood (shrimp, mussels, squid), optional
- ✓ 2 tbsp olive oil & Salt and pepper to taste
- ✓ Fresh cream and parsley for garnish

Step-by-Step Preparation:

1. In a large pot, heat the olive oil and sauté onions and garlic until translucent.
2. Add the pumpkin cubes and cook for about 5 minutes.
3. Pour in the stock and bring the mixture to a boil.
4. Once boiling, reduce heat and simmer until the pumpkin is tender.
5. Blend the soup mixture to a smooth consistency using an immersion or stand blender.
6. Add quinoa and simmer for another 15 minutes.
7. Stir in the spinach and seafood. Cook until the seafood is fully cooked and the spinach is wilted.
8. Season with salt and pepper.
9. Serve hot, garnished with a dash of fresh cream and parsley.

Nutritional Facts: (Per serving)

- ➢ Calories: 320
- ➢ Protein: 20g
- ➢ Carbohydrates: 45g
- ➢ Dietary Fiber: 8g
- ➢ Sugars: 6g
- ➢ Fat: 8g
- ➢ Sodium: 480mg

Melding the earthy flavors of pumpkin with the nourishing goodness of quinoa, spinach, and optional seafood, this Pumpkin Soup is more than a dish—a hearty, soul-warming experience. Every spoonful promises a particular seafood delight that'll leave you craving more.

Recipe 67: Beautiful Still Life of Boiled Corn

Experience the simple pleasure of the ocean's bounty with "Beautiful Still Life of Boiled Corn." This unexpected pairing of sweet corn with delicate seafood hints will transport you to a coastal haven right from your dining table.

Servings: 4

Prepping Time: 10 minutes

Cook Time: 20 minutes

Difficulty: Easy

Ingredients:

- 4 fresh corn cobs, husked
- 1-liter water
- 2 tsp sea salt
- 1 tsp seaweed flakes (like nori or doles)
- 2 tbsp unsalted butter

- ✓ 1 tbsp chopped parsley & Lemon wedges for serving

Step-by-Step Preparation:

1. In a large pot, bring water and sea salt to a boil.
2. Add the corn cobs and seaweed flakes.
3. Allow the corn to boil for 15-20 minutes or until tender.
4. Once cooked, remove the corn from the water and drain.
5. While still hot, brush each corn cob with unsalted butter.
6. Sprinkle with chopped parsley and serve with a wedge of lemon.

Nutritional Facts: (Per serving)

- ➢ Calories: 150
- ➢ Protein: 4g
- ➢ Carbohydrates: 32g
- ➢ Dietary Fiber: 3g
- ➢ Sugars: 7g
- ➢ Fat: 4g
- ➢ Sodium: 490mg

"Beautiful Still Life of Boiled Corn" isn't just a treat for the eyes but also an unexpected burst of flavors with every bite. With its hint of the sea from the seaweed flakes, this dish encapsulates the essence of Seafood Specials in a refreshingly unique way.

Recipe 68: Mahi Fish Sandwich with Salsa and Lettuce

Dive into the tantalizing taste of the ocean with the "Mahi Fish Sandwich with Salsa and Lettuce." This delightful dish combines the rich flavors of Mahi fish with the zest of fresh salsa, all tucked inside a soft bun for a complete seafood escapade.

Servings: 4

Prepping Time: 15 minutes

Cook Time: 20 minutes

Difficulty: Intermediate

Ingredients:

- 4 Mahi fish fillets
- 4 soft buns, split and toasted
- 2 cups fresh salsa (tomatoes, onions, cilantro, lime juice)
- 1 cup shredded lettuce
- 1 tbsp olive oil

- ✓ Salt and pepper to taste
- ✓ 1 tsp paprika
- ✓ 1 avocado, sliced
- ✓ 1 tbsp mayonnaise (optional)

Step-by-Step Preparation:

1. Season Mahi fish fillets with salt, pepper, and paprika.
2. Heat olive oil over medium-high heat in a skillet and sear the fillets for about 4 minutes on each side or until fully cooked.
3. Spread mayonnaise (if using) on each toasted bun half.
4. Place a fish fillet on the bottom half of each bun.
5. Top with fresh salsa, avocado slices, and shredded lettuce.
6. Complete with the top bun half and serve immediately.

Nutritional Facts: (Per serving)

- ➤ Calories: 380
- ➤ Protein: 34g
- ➤ Carbohydrates: 30g
- ➤ Dietary Fiber: 5g
- ➤ Sugars: 4g
- ➤ Fat: 12g
- ➤ Sodium: 680mg

The "Mahi Fish Sandwich with Salsa and Lettuce" is more than just a sandwich; it's a flavorful voyage of textures and tastes. Each bite offers a harmonious blend of succulent fish, zesty salsa, and crisp lettuce, promising an unforgettable Seafood Specials experience.

Recipe 69: Japanese Deep-Fried Crispy Tempura Prawn

Experience the exquisite simplicity of Japanese cuisine with "Japanese Deep-Fried Crispy Tempura Prawn." These light, airy, and golden delicacies bring out the true essence of the prawn, complemented by the delicate tempura batter.

Servings: 4

Prepping Time: 15 minutes

Cook Time: 10 minutes

Difficulty: Intermediate

Ingredients:

- 12 large fresh prawns, deveined and cleaned
- 1 cup tempura flour
- 1 cup cold sparkling water
- 1 tsp salt
- 1/2 tsp white pepper

- ✓ Vegetable oil for frying
- ✓ Lemon wedges for serving
- ✓ Dipping sauce

Step-by-Step Preparation:

1. Whisk together tempura flour, cold sparkling water, salt, and white pepper in a mixing bowl until smooth.
2. Heat vegetable oil in a deep-frying pan over medium-high heat.
3. Holding the prawns by the tail, dip them into the batter, ensuring they're fully coated.
4. Carefully drop the prawns into the hot oil and fry until golden brown, about 3-4 minutes.
5. Remove and drain on paper towels.
6. Serve hot with lemon wedges and dipping sauce.

Nutritional Facts: (Per serving)

- ➢ Calories: 220
- ➢ Protein: 12g
- ➢ Carbohydrates: 24g
- ➢ Dietary Fiber: 1g
- ➢ Sugars: 1g
- ➢ Fat: 8g
- ➢ Sodium: 720mg

The "Japanese Deep-Fried Crispy Tempura Prawn" offers an authentic taste of Japanese gastronomy. Every bite is a delightful crunch, revealing the succulent prawn within. Paired with a tangy dipping sauce, it's a Seafood special dish that captures the heart of culinary artistry.

Recipe 70: Roasted Fish with Almond and Salad

Delight in the refined flavors of the sea with "Roasted Fish with Almond and Salad." This sumptuous dish pairs perfectly roasted fish with the nutty richness of almonds and the fresh crunch of a hearty salad.

Servings: 4

Prepping Time: 20 minutes

Cook Time: 25 minutes

Difficulty: Intermediate

Ingredients:

- ✓ 4 fish fillets (such as cod or tilapia)
- ✓ 1/4 cup almonds, roughly chopped
- ✓ 2 tbsp olive oil
- ✓ Salt and pepper, to taste
- ✓ 4 cups mixed salad greens

- ✓ 1 lemon, zested and juiced
- ✓ 1/4 cup fresh parsley, chopped
- ✓ 2 tbsp balsamic vinegar

Step-by-Step Preparation:

1. Preheat oven to 400°F (200°C).
2. Rub fish fillets with olive oil, salt, and pepper.
3. Place fish on a baking sheet and sprinkle with chopped almonds.
4. Roast in the oven for 20-25 minutes or until the fish is flaky and almonds are golden.
5. Toss salad greens with lemon zest, juice, parsley, balsamic vinegar, and olive oil in a bowl.
6. Serve roasted fish atop a bed of fresh salad.

Nutritional Facts: (Per serving)

- ➢ Calories: 310
- ➢ Protein: 28g
- ➢ Carbohydrates: 6g
- ➢ Dietary Fiber: 3g
- ➢ Sugars: 2g
- ➢ Fat: 20g
- ➢ Sodium: 320mg

The "Roasted Fish with Almond and Salad" is a harmonious blend of textures and flavors. With every bite, you get the moist tenderness of the fish, the crunch of almonds, and the vibrant freshness of the salad. A Seafood Specials masterpiece for any occasion!

Chapter 08: Sip & Savor Smoothies

Recipe 71: Red and Pink Smoothies

Dive into the vibrant world of "Red and Pink Smoothies"! These delightful beverages offer a visual treat and a burst of natural flavors and nutrients, perfect for a rejuvenating Sip & Savor experience.

Servings: 2

Prepping Time: 10 minutes

Cook Time: 5 minutes

Difficulty: Easy

Ingredients:

- ✓ 1 cup strawberries, halved
- ✓ 1/2 cup raspberries
- ✓ 1/2 cup pomegranate seeds
- ✓ 1 banana, sliced

- ✓ 1 cup almond milk or yogurt
- ✓ 1 tbsp honey (optional)
- ✓ Ice cubes (optional)

Step-by-Step Preparation:

1. Wash and prepare the strawberries, raspberries, and pomegranate seeds.
2. Combine the strawberries, raspberries, bananas, and pomegranate seeds in a blender.
3. Pour in the almond milk or yogurt. Add honey if desired.
4. Blend until smooth, adding ice cubes for a colder smoothie.
5. Pour into glasses and serve immediately.

Nutritional Facts: (Per serving)

- ➢ Calories: 155
- ➢ Protein: 3g
- ➢ Carbohydrates: 35g
- ➢ Dietary Fiber: 6g
- ➢ Sugars: 24g
- ➢ Fat: 2g
- ➢ Sodium: 80mg

The "Red and Pink Smoothies" are not just a feast for the eyes but a nourishing sip packed with antioxidants and vitamins. Embrace this refreshing blend for a delightful Sip & Savor moment anytime you desire!

Recipe 72: Christmas Sugar Cookie White Russian Cocktail

Celebrate the festive season with the "Christmas Sugar Cookie White Russian Cocktail." This delightful concoction seamlessly merges the nostalgic taste of sugar cookies with the rich, creamy essence of a White Russian, making every sip a festive affair.

Servings: 2

Prepping Time: 10 minutes

Cook Time: 0 minutes

Difficulty: Easy

Ingredients:

- 4 oz vodka
- 2 oz coffee liqueur (e.g., Kahlua)
- 2 oz heavy cream or milk
- 1 tsp vanilla extract
- Sugar cookie crumbs (for rimming)

- ✓ Ice cubes
- ✓ Whipped cream (optional for topping)
- ✓ Christmas-themed sprinkles (optional)

Step-by-Step Preparation:

1. Wet the rim of the serving glasses and dip into sugar cookie crumbs.
2. Combine vodka, coffee liqueur, heavy cream or milk, and vanilla extract in a cocktail shaker.
3. Fill the shaker with ice cubes and shake until well-mixed.
4. Strain the cocktail into the prepared glasses.
5. Top with whipped cream and Christmas-themed sprinkles if desired.

Nutritional Facts: (Per serving)

- ➢ Calories: 315
- ➢ Protein: 1g
- ➢ Carbohydrates: 18g
- ➢ Sugars: 16g
- ➢ Fat: 9g
- ➢ Sodium: 15mg

Let the "Christmas Sugar Cookie White Russian Cocktail" transport you to a winter wonderland. It's the perfect drink to raise a toast to the magic of the season, making every Sip & Savor moment genuinely enchanting.

Recipe 73: Energy Berry Bliss Balls of Desiccated Coconut Mixed

Experience a burst of natural vitality with "Energy Berry Bliss Balls," where the tartness of berries beautifully marries the tropical allure of desiccated coconut. Perfect for those on-the-go moments, these balls are your pocket-sized energy boost.

Servings: 12 balls

Prepping Time: 15 minutes

Cook Time: 0 minutes

Difficulty: Easy

Ingredients:

- ✓ 1 cup mixed berries (frozen or fresh)
- ✓ 1 cup desiccated coconut
- ✓ 1/2 cup rolled oats
- ✓ 1/4 cup honey or maple syrup

- ✓ 1 tsp vanilla extract
- ✓ A pinch of salt

Step-by-Step Preparation:

1. Combine mixed berries, oats, half of the desiccated coconut, honey, vanilla extract, and salt in a food processor.
2. Process until the mixture is well combined and slightly sticky.
3. Shape the mixture into small balls using your hands.
4. Roll the balls in the remaining desiccated coconut to coat them evenly.
5. Please place them in the refrigerator for at least an hour to set.

Nutritional Facts: (Per serving)

- ➢ Calories: 105
- ➢ Protein: 1.5g
- ➢ Carbohydrates: 14g
- ➢ Sugars: 8g
- ➢ Fat: 5g
- ➢ Sodium: 5mg

"Energy Berry Bliss Balls" are more than just a treat; they're a wholesome solution to mid-day slumps. Every bite carries the promise of sustained energy and pure Sip & Savor deliciousness. Enjoy them anytime you need a lift!

Recipe 74: Hot Mocha Coffee

Dive into a mug of "Hot Mocha Coffee," a dreamy blend of rich coffee and indulgent chocolate. It's a luxurious upgrade to your regular coffee routine, a comforting concoction that offers warmth on chilly mornings or evenings.

Servings: 2 cups

Prepping Time: 5 minutes

Cook Time: 5 minutes

Difficulty: Easy

Ingredients:

- ✓ 2 cups freshly brewed coffee
- ✓ 1/2 cup whole milk
- ✓ 2 tbsp unsweetened cocoa powder
- ✓ 3 tbsp sugar (adjust to taste)
- ✓ Whipped cream (optional for topping)
- ✓ Chocolate shavings or cocoa for garnish

Step-by-Step Preparation:

1. In a saucepan, heat milk, but don't bring it to a boil.
2. Add cocoa powder and sugar, whisking continuously to avoid lumps.
3. Pour the brewed coffee into the milk mixture and stir well.
4. Heat the mocha mixture until it's hot but not boiling.
5. Pour into mugs, top with whipped cream if desired, and garnish with chocolate shavings or a sprinkle of cocoa.

Nutritional Facts: (Per serving)

- Calories: 90
- Protein: 2g
- Carbohydrates: 18g
- Sugars: 12g
- Fat: 1.5g
- Sodium: 25mg

The "Hot Mocha Coffee" is more than just a beverage—it's a moment of pure indulgence. Perfect for those looking for a touch of decadence in their Sip & Savor experience, it promises warmth, comfort, and sweetness in every sip.

Recipe 75: Trendy Comfort Snack Crispy Roasted Crushed Potatoes

Dive into the latest snacking trend with "Trendy Comfort Snack Crispy Roasted Crushed Potatoes." These golden-brown delights contrast textures: a crunchy exterior and a soft, fluffy inside. Perfect as a snack or side dish, they're the epitome of modern comfort food.

Servings: 4

Prepping Time: 15 minutes

Cook Time: 45 minutes

Difficulty: Medium

Ingredients:

- ✓ 8 smalls to medium-sized potatoes
- ✓ 3 tbsp olive oil
- ✓ Salt, to taste
- ✓ 2 tsp black pepper

- ✓ 2 tsp rosemary (fresh or dried)
- ✓ 2 cloves of garlic, minced

Step-by-Step Preparation:

1. Preheat the oven to 425°F (220°C).
2. Boil potatoes in salted water until they're tender but not falling apart.
3. Drain and allow to cool slightly.
4. On a baking sheet, place each potato and gently press down to crush them without completely breaking apart.
5. Drizzle olive oil over the potatoes.
6. Sprinkle minced garlic, rosemary, salt, and black pepper evenly.
7. Roast in the oven until crispy and golden, about 25-30 minutes.

Nutritional Facts: (Per serving)

- ➢ Calories: 210
- ➢ Protein: 4g
- ➢ Carbohydrates: 40g
- ➢ Dietary Fiber: 3g
- ➢ Sugars: 2g
- ➢ Fat: 5g
- ➢ Sodium: 10mg

The "Trendy Comfort Snack Crispy Roasted Crushed Potatoes" perfectly encapsulates what Sip & Savor is all about comfort with a trendy twist. These potatoes are not just food but an experience of textures and flavors that bring warmth and joy in every bite. Indulge and enjoy!

Recipe 76: Making Juice with Mango Fruit

Brighten up your day with a refreshing "Juice with Mango Fruit." This sweet, tropical delight quenches your thirst and transports you to a sun-kissed beach with each sip. It's the epitome of liquid sunshine.

Servings: 2

Prepping Time: 10 minutes

Cook Time: 0 minutes

Difficulty: Easy

Ingredients:

- ✓ 2 ripe mangoes, peeled and pitted
- ✓ 1 cup of cold water
- ✓ 1 tbsp honey (optional)
- ✓ Ice cubes
- ✓ A splash of lime juice (optional)
- ✓ Mint leaves for garnish (optional)

Step-by-Step Preparation:

1. Combine the mango flesh, cold water, and honey in a blender.
2. Blend until smooth and creamy.
3. Taste and adjust sweetness, if necessary. Add a splash of lime juice for a hint of tanginess if desired.
4. Pour into glasses over ice cubes.
5. Garnish with mint leaves if using.

Nutritional Facts: (Per serving)

- Calories: 120
- Protein: 1g
- Carbohydrates: 30g
- Dietary Fiber: 3g
- Sugars: 27g
- Fat: 0.5g
- Sodium: 3mg

Experience the taste of tropical paradise in every glass of "Juice with Mango Fruit." Perfect for hot days or when you need a fruity pick-me-up, this Sip & Savor specialty captures the essence of summer in its purest form. Cheers to vibrant flavors and sunlit moments!

Recipe 77: Beautifully Decorated Muffins

Elevate your tea-time experience with "Beautifully Decorated Muffins". Crafted with love and adorned with tempting toppings, these muffins are more than just a treat - they're a visual feast. Dive into a world where taste meets artistry in every bite.

Servings: 6

Prepping Time: 15 minutes

Cook Time: 20 minutes

Difficulty: Intermediate

Ingredients:

- ✓ 2 cups all-purpose flour
- ✓ 1 cup sugar
- ✓ 1/2 cup unsalted butter, softened
- ✓ 2 large eggs
- ✓ 1 cup milk

- ✓ 2 tsp baking powder
- ✓ 1 tsp vanilla extract
- ✓ Assorted toppings: chocolate chips, berries, edible flowers, and drizzled icing

Step-by-Step Preparation:

1. Preheat oven to 375°F (190°C) and line a muffin tray with paper liners.
2. In a mixing bowl, cream together butter and sugar until fluffy.
3. Beat in the eggs one at a time, then stir in vanilla.
4. Combine the flour and baking powder; add to the creamed mixture alternately with milk.
5. Fill muffin cups 2/3 full.
6. Bake for 20 minutes or until a toothpick comes out clean.
7. Allow to cool and decorate with your choice of toppings.

Nutritional Facts: (Per serving)

- ➢ Calories: 320
- ➢ Protein: 5g
- ➢ Carbohydrates: 50g
- ➢ Dietary Fiber: 1g
- ➢ Sugars: 25g
- ➢ Fat: 12g
- ➢ Sodium: 150mg

"Beautifully Decorated Muffins" are a delight to the palate and a feast for the eyes. Perfect for special occasions or when you're looking to indulge, these Sip & Savor gems bring art to the table, one muffin at a time. Celebrate life's sweet moments with elegance and flavor!

Recipe 78: Grilled Chicken with Rice

Unleash the symphony of flavors with "Grilled Chicken with Rice." This classic duo gets a Sip & Savor twist, blending hearty grilled chicken with perfectly cooked fluffy rice. Ideal for any meal, it's the harmony of simplicity and taste in every bite.

Servings: 4

Prepping Time: 15 minutes

Cook Time: 40 minutes

Difficulty: Easy

Ingredients:

- 4 boneless, skinless chicken breasts
- 2 cups long-grain rice, washed and drained
- 4 cups chicken broth
- 2 tbsp olive oil
- 1 tsp garlic powder

- ✓ 1 tsp onion powder
- ✓ Salt and pepper to taste
- ✓ Fresh herbs for garnish (optional)

Step-by-Step Preparation:

1. Preheat the grill to medium-high heat.
2. Season chicken breasts with garlic, onion, salt, and pepper.
3. Drizzle olive oil over the chicken and place on the grill. Cook for 6-7 minutes per side or until fully cooked.
4. In a saucepan, bring chicken broth to a boil. Add rice, reduce heat to low, cover, and simmer for 20 minutes or until rice is tender.
5. Serve grilled chicken over rice and garnish with fresh herbs if desired.

Nutritional Facts: (Per serving)

- ➤ Calories: 430
- ➤ Protein: 35g
- ➤ Carbohydrates: 50g
- ➤ Dietary Fiber: 1g
- ➤ Sugars: 1g
- ➤ Fat: 10g
- ➤ Sodium: 250mg

Relish the comfort of "Grilled Chicken with Rice," a timeless favorite revamped for the modern palate. With the signature Sip & Savor flair, this dish is nourishing and delicious, making every meal a delightful experience. Elevate your dining moments with this delectable pairing!

Recipe 79: Baked Chicken with Fruits and Greens

Embark on a culinary journey with "Baked Chicken with Fruits and Greens." This Sip & Savor creation melds the succulence of baked chicken with the fresh vibrancy of fruits and greens, crafting an entree that's both wholesome and indulgent. It's a refreshing spin on a classic dish.

Servings: 4

Prepping Time: 20 minutes

Cook Time: 45 minutes

Difficulty: Moderate

Ingredients:

- 4 boneless, skinless chicken breasts
- 2 cups mixed fruits (e.g., sliced apples, grapes, and berries)
- 3 cups mixed greens (e.g., spinach, arugula, and kale)
- 3 tbsp olive oil

- ✓ 1 tsp rosemary, finely chopped
- ✓ 2 garlic cloves, minced
- ✓ Salt and pepper to taste
- ✓ 1/4 cup balsamic vinaigrette

Step-by-Step Preparation:

1. Preheat oven to 375°F (190°C).
2. Rub chicken breasts with olive oil, garlic, rosemary, salt, and pepper.
3. Place chicken in a baking dish and bake for 25-30 minutes or until fully cooked.
4. In a large bowl, mix fruits and greens.
5. Slice the baked chicken and place atop the fruit and greens mixture.
6. Drizzle with balsamic vinaigrette before serving.

Nutritional Facts: (Per serving)

- ➢ Calories: 320
- ➢ Protein: 30g
- ➢ Carbohydrates: 20g
- ➢ Dietary Fiber: 4g
- ➢ Sugars: 14g
- ➢ Fat: 12g
- ➢ Sodium: 220mg

Dive into the delightful blend of flavors in "Baked Chicken with Fruits and Greens," a testament to Sip & Savor's commitment to innovation and taste. This dish promises a melody of savory, sweet, and fresh notes, elevating your dining experience to new heights. Enjoy the harmony of nature's best with every bite!

Recipe 80: Fresh Baked Chocolate Rolls

Indulge in the sweet allure of "Fresh Baked Chocolate Rolls," a Sip & Savor delicacy that dances between comfort food and luxurious treats. The warm chocolate unfurls its richness with every bite, making it an irresistible charm for all occasions.

Servings: 8

Prepping Time: 20 minutes

Cook Time: 25 minutes

Difficulty: Moderate

Ingredients:

- ✓ 2 cups all-purpose flour
- ✓ 2 tsp baking powder
- ✓ 1/2 tsp salt
- ✓ 1/3 cup unsweetened cocoa powder
- ✓ 1/2 cup granulated sugar

- ✓ 3/4 cup milk
- ✓ 1/4 cup melted butter
- ✓ 1 cup chocolate chips

Step-by-Step Preparation:

1. Preheat the oven to 375°F (190°C).
2. Whisk together flour, baking powder, salt, cocoa powder, and sugar in a large bowl.
3. Add milk and melted butter to the mixture and stir until combined.
4. Roll out the dough and sprinkle with chocolate chips.
5. Roll up tightly and slice into 8 pieces.
6. Place rolls on a baking sheet and bake for 25 minutes or until golden.

Nutritional Facts: (Per serving)

- ➤ Calories: 290
- ➤ Protein: 4g
- ➤ Carbohydrates: 52g
- ➤ Dietary Fiber: 2g
- ➤ Sugars: 28g
- ➤ Fat: 9g
- ➤ Sodium: 210mg

The "Fresh Baked Chocolate Rolls" showcase Sip & Savor's ability to craft treats that tantalize the taste buds and warm the heart. Perfect for morning tea, dessert, or any time you crave a chocolatey delight, these rolls will become a cherished recipe in your collection. Relish the fusion of simplicity and elegance!

Chapter 09: Salad Satisfiers

Recipe 81: Grilled Chicken Breast in Different Variation

Discover the versatile charm of "Grilled Chicken Breast in Different Variations," a highlight in the Salad Satisfiers series. Elevate your salads with chicken variations that are both flavorful and succulent, ensuring every meal is both healthy and satiating.

Servings: 4

Prepping Time: 15 minutes

Cook Time: 20 minutes

Difficulty: Easy

Ingredients:

- ✓ 4 boneless, skinless chicken breasts
- ✓ 2 tbsp olive oil

- ✓ 1 tsp garlic powder
- ✓ 1 tsp onion powder
- ✓ Salt and pepper to taste
- ✓ 1 tbsp fresh lemon juice
- ✓ Fresh herbs (rosemary, thyme, oregano) for variations

Step-by-Step Preparation:

1. Preheat the grill to medium-high heat.
2. Rub chicken breasts with olive oil, garlic powder, onion powder, salt, and pepper.
3. Grill chicken for 7-10 minutes on each side or until fully cooked.
4. For variations, sprinkle with different combinations of fresh herbs or drizzle with lemon juice before serving.

Nutritional Facts: (Per serving)

- ➤ Calories: 165
- ➤ Protein: 28g
- ➤ Carbohydrates: 1g
- ➤ Dietary Fiber: 0g
- ➤ Sugars: 0g
- ➤ Fat: 6g
- ➤ Sodium: 70mg

With "Grilled Chicken Breast in Different Variations" from Salad Satisfiers, you can add gourmet to your everyday salads. Simple yet brimming with flavors, these variations guarantee a delightful culinary journey. Mix and match to find your favorite, or introduce a new twist every time!

Recipe 82: Delicious Mediterranean Green Shakshuka Fried with Eggs

Dive into the rich flavors of the Mediterranean with "Delicious Mediterranean Green Shakshuka Fried with Eggs." As a prime feature in the Salad Satisfiers series, this dish combines wholesome greens and creamy eggs for a satisfying, nutrient-packed meal.

Servings: 4

Prepping Time: 10 minutes

Cook Time: 20 minutes

Difficulty: Intermediate

Ingredients:

- ✓ 2 tbsp olive oil
- ✓ 1 onion, finely chopped
- ✓ 2 cloves garlic, minced
- ✓ 4 cups mixed greens (spinach, kale, chard)

- ✓ 4 large eggs
- ✓ 1 tsp cumin
- ✓ Salt and pepper to taste
- ✓ 1/4 cup feta cheese (optional)
- ✓ Fresh herbs for garnish

Step-by-Step Preparation:

1. Heat olive oil in a skillet over medium heat.
2. Sauté onion and garlic until translucent.
3. Add mixed greens, cumin, salt, and pepper, cooking until greens are wilted.
4. Make wells in the gardens and crack the eggs into each well.
5. Cover and cook until eggs are set to your liking.
6. Garnish with feta cheese and fresh herbs if desired.

Nutritional Facts: (Per serving)

- ➤ Calories: 190
- ➤ Protein: 9g
- ➤ Carbohydrates: 8g
- ➤ Dietary Fiber: 2g
- ➤ Sugars: 2g
- ➤ Fat: 14g
- ➤ Sodium: 190mg

Let the "Delicious Mediterranean Green Shakshuka Fried with Eggs" from Salad Satisfiers whisk you away to sun-soaked Mediterranean shores. Perfect for brunch or a light dinner, every bite of this dish offers a delightful balance of earthy greens and rich eggs, creating a symphony of textures and flavors.

Recipe 83: Soft Focus Raw Beef Spicy Minced Meat Salad

Discover a fusion of flavor and texture with "Soft Focus Raw Beef Spicy Minced Meat Salad." This Salad Satisfiers' dish elevates the traditional salad experience, blending tender beef with a burst of spice for a gourmet delight.

Servings: 4

Prepping Time: 15 minutes

Cook Time: 0 minutes (Raw)

Difficulty: Easy

Ingredients:

- ✓ 400g high-quality beef, minced
- ✓ 2 fresh red chilies, finely sliced
- ✓ 2 tbsp lime juice
- ✓ 3 tbsp fish sauce
- ✓ 2 tsp sugar

- ✓ 1 small red onion, thinly sliced
- ✓ Fresh cilantro and mint leaves, chopped
- ✓ Toasted rice powder (optional)

Step-by-Step Preparation:

1. Combine lime juice, fish sauce, and sugar in a mixing bowl until well combined.
2. Add minced beef, chilies, and red onion to the bowl and mix thoroughly.
3. Allow the mixture to marinate for about 10 minutes.
4. Toss in fresh cilantro, mint leaves, and toasted rice powder.
5. Serve immediately.

Nutritional Facts: (Per serving)

- ➢ Calories: 220
- ➢ Protein: 20g
- ➢ Carbohydrates: 4g
- ➢ Dietary Fiber: 0.5g
- ➢ Sugars: 3g
- ➢ Fat: 13g
- ➢ Sodium: 580mg

The "Soft Focus Raw Beef Spicy Minced Meat Salad" brings an innovative touch to Salad Satisfiers. Perfect for those looking to venture beyond traditional salads, this dish promises a refreshing blend of spice, zest, and juiciness, setting the tone for a memorable dining affair.

Recipe 84: Peppers Grill Baked Vegetable Pepper Grilled

Experience a medley of colorful and tantalizing flavors with the "Peppers Grill Baked Vegetable Pepper Grilled" dish. Perfect for those craving a wholesome and vibrant treat, this Salad Satisfiers recipe embodies the essence of grilled perfection.

Servings: 4

Prepping Time: 10 minutes

Cook Time: 20 minutes

Difficulty: Easy

Ingredients:

- 4 large bell peppers (red, yellow, green, orange), halved and deseeded
- 2 tbsp olive oil
- 2 cloves garlic, minced
- 1 tsp dried oregano

- ✓ Salt and pepper to taste
- ✓ 1/4 cup grated Parmesan cheese
- ✓ Fresh basil leaves for garnish

Step-by-Step Preparation:

1. Preheat the grill to medium heat.
2. Mix olive oil, garlic, oregano, salt, and pepper in a bowl.
3. Brush the mixture over the insides of the bell pepper halves.
4. Place peppers on the grill cut side down, and cook for 10 minutes.
5. Flip and sprinkle with Parmesan cheese, grilling for another 10 minutes or until tender.
6. Garnish with fresh basil leaves before serving.

Nutritional Facts: (Per serving)

- ➢ Calories: 110
- ➢ Protein: 3g
- ➢ Carbohydrates: 7g
- ➢ Dietary Fiber: 2g
- ➢ Sugars: 4g
- ➢ Fat: 7g
- ➢ Sodium: 120mg

The vibrant "Peppers Grill Baked Vegetable Pepper Grilled" dish satisfies your salad cravings. A celebration of grilled textures and rich flavors, this Salad Satisfiers specialty will surely be the star of any meal, offering nutrition and gastronomic delight.

Recipe 85: Tuscan Bean and Tuna Salad with Tomatoes

Dive into the rustic flavors of Tuscany with the "Tuscan Bean and Tuna Salad with Tomatoes." This Salad Satisfiers' dish elegantly marries hearty beans with the freshness of tuna and tomatoes, offering a taste of the Mediterranean in every bite.

Servings: 4

Prepping Time: 15 minutes

Cook Time: 0 minutes

Difficulty: Easy

Ingredients:

- 1 can (15 oz) cannellini beans, drained and rinsed
- 1 can (6 oz) tuna in olive oil, drained and flaked
- 2 cups cherry tomatoes, halved
- 1/4 cup fresh parsley, chopped

- ✓ 2 tbsp olive oil
- ✓ 1 tbsp red wine vinegar
- ✓ Salt and pepper to taste
- ✓ 1 garlic clove, minced
- ✓ Grated zest of 1 lemon

Step-by-Step Preparation:

1. Combine cannellini beans, flaked tuna, and halved cherry tomatoes in a large mixing bowl.
2. Whisk together olive oil, red wine vinegar, garlic, lemon zest, salt, and pepper in a separate smaller bowl to create the dressing.
3. Pour the dressing over the bean and tuna mixture.
4. Add chopped parsley and gently toss to combine.
5. Adjust seasoning if needed and serve chilled.

Nutritional Facts: (Per serving)

- ➢ Calories: 240
- ➢ Protein: 18g
- ➢ Carbohydrates: 22g
- ➢ Dietary Fiber: 6g
- ➢ Sugars: 3g
- ➢ Fat: 8g
- ➢ Sodium: 350mg

Transport your palate to the heart of Italy with the "Tuscan Bean and Tuna Salad with Tomatoes." Ideal for health enthusiasts seeking depth of flavor, this Salad Satisfiers specialty delivers a balanced combination of nutrition and classic Mediterranean charm.

Recipe 86: Healthy Tempeh Tacos Dripping

Elevate your taco game with "Healthy Tempeh Tacos Dripping." A Salad Satisfier's favorite, these tacos blend the nutty taste of tempeh with fresh, vibrant toppings, making them wholesome and utterly irresistible.

Servings: 4

Prepping Time: 20 minutes

Cook Time: 10 minutes

Difficulty: Medium

Ingredients:

- ✓ 8 oz tempeh, crumbled
- ✓ 8 small corn tortillas
- ✓ 2 tbsp olive oil
- ✓ 1 tsp cumin powder
- ✓ 1 tsp smoked paprika
- ✓ 1/2 cup fresh salsa

- ✓ 1 avocado, sliced
- ✓ 1/4 cup fresh cilantro, chopped
- ✓ 1 lime, cut into wedges
- ✓ Salt and pepper to taste

Step-by-Step Preparation:

1. In a skillet, heat the olive oil over medium heat. Add the crumbled tempeh and cook until golden brown.
2. Sprinkle cumin powder, smoked paprika, salt, and pepper over the tempeh. Stir well.
3. Warm the corn tortillas in a separate pan or oven.
4. Assemble the tacos by placing tempeh on each tortilla, followed by salsa, avocado slices, and cilantro.
5. Serve with lime wedges on the side for a zesty kick.

Nutritional Facts: (Per serving)

- ➢ Calories: 320
- ➢ Protein: 14g
- ➢ Carbohydrates: 35g
- ➢ Dietary Fiber: 7g
- ➢ Sugars: 4g
- ➢ Fat: 16g
- ➢ Sodium: 280mg

The "Healthy Tempeh Tacos Dripping" is not just another taco dish; it's a symphony of flavors celebrating health and taste. Perfect for a quick dinner or a gathering, these Salad Satisfiers' tacos will leave everyone craving for more.

Recipe 87: Chickpea Soup Moroccan Traditional Dish

Dive into the exotic flavors of North Africa with the "Chickpea Soup Moroccan Traditional Dish." A quintessential Salad Satisfier pick, this soup is a heart-warming blend of chickpeas and aromatic spices, promising a culinary journey to the Moroccan streets.

Servings: 4

Prepping Time: 15 minutes

Cook Time: 40 minutes

Difficulty: Medium

Ingredients:

- 2 cups dried chickpeas, soaked overnight
- 1 large onion, finely chopped
- 3 cloves garlic, minced
- 1 tsp ground cumin

- ✓ 1 tsp ground turmeric
- ✓ 1 tsp paprika
- ✓ 1/2 tsp ground cinnamon
- ✓ 4 cups vegetable broth
- ✓ 2 tbsp olive oil
- ✓ Salt and pepper to taste
- ✓ Fresh parsley and lemon wedges for garnish

Step-by-Step Preparation:

1. In a large pot, heat olive oil over medium heat. Sauté onions until translucent.
2. Add garlic, cumin, turmeric, paprika, and cinnamon. Stir for 1-2 minutes until aromatic.
3. Add the soaked chickpeas and vegetable broth. Bring to a boil.
4. Reduce heat, cover, and simmer for 35-40 minutes or until chickpeas are tender.
5. Season with salt and pepper. Serve hot, garnished with fresh parsley and a squeeze of lemon.

Nutritional Facts: (Per serving)

- ➢ Calories: 280
- ➢ Protein: 14g
- ➢ Carbohydrates: 45g
- ➢ Dietary Fiber: 12g
- ➢ Sugars: 8g
- ➢ Fat: 7g
- ➢ Sodium: 600mg

The "Chickpea Soup Moroccan Traditional Dish" is a flavorful escapade to the heart of Morocco. This Salad Satisfiers soup offers both nourishment and a delightful taste expedition.

Recipe 88: Avocado Greek Yogurt Sauce

Unveil the perfect fusion of creaminess and zest with the "Avocado Greek Yogurt Sauce." This Salad Satisfiers dish is a delightful dip and a versatile spread, bringing texture and flavor to your culinary adventures.

Servings: 4

Prepping Time: 10 minutes

Cook Time: 0 minutes (No cooking required)

Difficulty: Easy

Ingredients:

- ✓ 2 ripe avocados, peeled and pitted
- ✓ 1 cup Greek yogurt
- ✓ 2 cloves garlic, minced
- ✓ Juice of 1 lime
- ✓ 2 tbsp fresh cilantro, chopped
- ✓ Salt and pepper to taste

Step-by-Step Preparation:

1. Combine avocados, Greek yogurt, garlic, and lime juice in a blender or food processor.
2. Blend until smooth and creamy.
3. Add chopped cilantro and blend briefly to incorporate.
4. Season with salt and pepper to taste.
5. Transfer to a bowl and refrigerate before serving.

Nutritional Facts: (Per serving)

- Calories: 190
- Protein: 5g
- Carbohydrates: 12g
- Dietary Fiber: 7g
- Sugars: 2g
- Fat: 15g
- Sodium: 25mg

Elevate your salads, sandwiches, or grilled dishes with the luscious "Avocado Greek Yogurt Sauce." As a Salad Satisfier choice, it's a symphony of flavors, making every meal an unforgettable experience.

Recipe 89: Spicy Southwestern Chicken Salad

Dive into the vibrant and zesty world of the "Spicy Southwestern Chicken Salad." This Salad Satisfiers dish is a delightful homage to Southwestern flavors, a delectable fusion of juicy chicken, fresh veggies, and a kick of spice.

Servings: 4

Prepping Time: 20 minutes

Cook Time: 15 minutes

Difficulty: Moderate

Ingredients:

- ✓ 2 boneless chicken breasts
- ✓ 1 cup black beans, rinsed and drained
- ✓ 1 cup corn kernels
- ✓ 1 red bell pepper, diced
- ✓ 2 green onions, sliced
- ✓ 1/4 cup fresh cilantro, chopped

- ✓ 1 avocado, diced
- ✓ 1 tsp chili powder
- ✓ Salt and pepper to taste
- ✓ 2 tbsp olive oil
- ✓ Juice of 1 lime

Step-by-Step Preparation:

1. Season chicken breasts with chili powder, salt, and pepper.
2. In a skillet, heat olive oil and cook chicken until browned and cooked through.
3. Slice cooked chicken into thin strips.
4. Combine chicken strips, black beans, corn, bell pepper, green onions, and cilantro in a large bowl.
5. Drizzle with lime juice and gently toss.
6. Garnish with diced avocado before serving.

Nutritional Facts: (Per serving)

- ➢ Calories: 330
- ➢ Protein: 28g
- ➢ Carbohydrates: 22g
- ➢ Dietary Fiber: 7g
- ➢ Sugars: 4g
- ➢ Fat: 15g
- ➢ Sodium: 240mg

Embrace the bold and hearty essence of the "Spicy Southwestern Chicken Salad." Perfect for those seeking a burst of flavor and a fulfilling meal, this Salad Satisfiers dish will undoubtedly become a go-to favorite.

Recipe 90: Sliced Steak of Tuna in Sesame and a Salad

Indulge in the refined flavors of the "Sliced Steak of Tuna in Sesame and a Salad." This Salad Satisfiers dish elegantly marries the richness of tuna with the nuttiness of sesame, all complemented by a crisp salad.

Servings: 4

Prepping Time: 15 minutes

Cook Time: 10 minutes

Difficulty: Moderate

Ingredients:

- ✓ 4 fresh tuna steaks
- ✓ 1/2 cup sesame seeds (black and white mix)
- ✓ 2 tbsp soy sauce
- ✓ 2 tbsp olive oil
- ✓ 4 cups mixed salad greens

- ✓ 1/4 cup cherry tomatoes, halved
- ✓ 1/2 cucumber, thinly sliced
- ✓ 1/4 cup red onion, thinly sliced
- ✓ 2 tbsp sesame oil
- ✓ Juice of 1 lemon

Step-by-Step Preparation:

1. Coat the tuna steaks with soy sauce and let them marinate for 5 minutes.
2. Spread sesame seeds on a plate and press each side of the tuna steaks into the roots.
3. In a skillet, heat olive oil and sear the tuna steaks for 2-3 minutes each side.
4. Combine salad greens, tomatoes, cucumber, and red onion in a large bowl.
5. Drizzle with sesame oil and lemon juice, tossing gently.
6. Slice the seared tuna and place atop the salad.

Nutritional Facts: (Per serving)

- ➤ Calories: 370
- ➤ Protein: 28g
- ➤ Carbohydrates: 12g
- ➤ Dietary Fiber: 4g
- ➤ Sugars: 3g
- ➤ Fat: 24g
- ➤ Sodium: 340mg

Relish the exquisite dance of flavors in the "Sliced Steak of Tuna in Sesame and a Salad." This dish is a Salad Satisfiers gem that brings a symphony of textures and tastes, perfect for an elegant lunch or dinner.

Chapter 10: Dessert Decadence

Recipe 91: Chocolate Cake & Cream

Dive into the delightful layers of "Chocolate Cake with Protein Peach Cream." A Dessert Decadence offering, this cake combines the indulgence of chocolate with the refreshing twist of protein-packed peach cream for a truly irresistible treat.

Servings: 8

Prepping Time: 25 minutes

Cook Time: 30 minutes

Difficulty: Intermediate

Ingredients:

- ✓ 2 cups all-purpose flour & 1 cup unsweetened cocoa powder
- ✓ 1 1/2 cups granulated sugar & 2 tsp baking powder
- ✓ 1/2 tsp salt & 1 cup milk
- ✓ 1/2 cup unsalted butter, melted & 2 large eggs & 1 tsp vanilla extract

- **For the Protein Peach Cream:**
  - 2 ripe peaches, peeled and pureed
  - 1 cup Greek yogurt & 2 tbsp honey
  - 1 scoop vanilla protein powder

Step-by-Step Preparation:

1. Preheat oven to 350°F (175°C). Grease and flour a cake tin.
2. Sift flour, cocoa powder, sugar, baking powder, and salt in a large bowl.
3. Mix in milk, melted butter, eggs, and vanilla until smooth.
4. Pour batter into the prepared tin and bake for 30 minutes or until a toothpick comes out clean.
5. While the cake cools, combine peach puree, Greek yogurt, honey, and protein powder to make the peach cream.
6. Once the cake is cooled, spread the protein peach cream over the top.

Nutritional Facts: (Per serving)

- Calories: 320
- Protein: 12g
- Carbohydrates: 45g
- Dietary Fiber: 3g
- Sugars: 28g
- Fat: 12g
- Sodium: 150mg

Celebrate the joy of sweet indulgence paired with a nutritious punch in the "Chocolate Cake with Protein Peach Cream." A Dessert Decadence in particular, this cake is a delightful end to a grand meal or a luxurious treat for any time of the day.

Recipe 92: Lemon Cheesecake

Unveil the zesty allure of the "Lemon Cheesecake on Wooden Board." A Dessert Decadence masterpiece, this cheesecake boasts a creamy texture bursting with tangy lemon flavors, all served on an authentic wooden board for an added rustic charm.

Servings: 10

Prepping Time: 20 minutes

Cook Time: 50 minutes

Difficulty: Intermediate

Ingredients:

- 1 1/2 cups graham cracker crumbs
- 1/4 cup unsalted butter, melted
- 4 cups cream cheese, softened
- 1 cup granulated sugar
- 4 large eggs
- Zest and juice of 2 lemons

- ✓ 1 tsp vanilla extract
- ✓ Pinch of salt

Step-by-Step Preparation:

1. Preheat oven to 325°F (163°C).
2. Mix graham cracker crumbs and melted butter press into the base of a springform pan.
3. In a separate bowl, beat cream cheese and sugar until smooth.
4. Incorporate eggs one at a time, followed by lemon zest, juice, vanilla, and salt.
5. Pour mixture over crust and bake for 50 minutes or until just set.
6. Cool and refrigerate for 4 hours or overnight before serving on a wooden board.

Nutritional Facts: (Per serving)

- ➢ Calories: 410
- ➢ Protein: 7g
- ➢ Carbohydrates: 30g
- ➢ Dietary Fiber: 0.5g
- ➢ Sugars: 25g
- ➢ Fat: 30g
- ➢ Sodium: 250mg

Indulge in a slice of heavenly "Lemon Cheesecake on Wooden Board," blending tart and creamy notes perfectly. A signature of Dessert Decadence, this cheesecake promises to elevate any dining experience with its delectable charm.

Recipe 93: Mousse Cake Made of Chocolate

Indulge in the luxurious experience of the Mousse Cake Made of Chocolate. This Dessert Decadence delight showcases velvety chocolate layers that melt in the mouth, making every bite a testament to sweet perfection.

Servings: 8

Prepping Time: 25 minutes

Cook Time: 20 minutes (plus refrigeration time)

Difficulty: Intermediate

Ingredients:

- 200g dark chocolate, chopped
- 3 large eggs, separated
- 1/4 cup granulated sugar
- 1 tsp vanilla extract
- 1 cup heavy cream
- Pinch of salt & Cocoa powder for dusting

Step-by-Step Preparation:

1. Melt the chocolate in a heatproof bowl set over a pot of simmering water. Remove from heat and cool slightly.
2. Whisk egg yolks, sugar, and vanilla until creamy. Gradually mix in the melted chocolate.
3. Whip the egg whites with a pinch of salt in a separate bowl until stiff peaks form.
4. Gently fold the egg whites into the chocolate mixture.
5. Whip the heavy cream in another bowl until stiff and fold it into the chocolate-egg mixture.
6. Pour into a cake mold and refrigerate for at least 6 hours or until set.
7. Before serving, dust with cocoa powder.

Nutritional Facts: (Per serving)

- Calories: 320
- Protein: 6g
- Carbohydrates: 22g
- Dietary Fiber: 2g
- Sugars: 18g
- Fat: 24g
- Sodium: 60mg

A symphony of flavors awaits with the "Mousse Cake Made of Chocolate." This Dessert Decadence creation is a must-try for all who seek the epitome of chocolatey indulgence.

Recipe 94: Asty Chocolate Wedding Cake Decorated with Berries

Celebrate the union of two souls with the "Tasty Chocolate Wedding Cake Decorated with Berries." This Dessert Decadence masterpiece, rich in flavors and adorned with vibrant berries, promises to be the showstopper at any matrimonial feast.

Servings: 50

Prepping Time: 3 hours

Cook Time: 40 minutes

Difficulty: Expert

Ingredients:

- ✓ 500g dark chocolate, chopped
- ✓ 400g unsalted butter
- ✓ 700g granulated sugar
- ✓ 10 large eggs
- ✓ 600g all-purpose flour

- ✓ 3 tsp baking powder
- ✓ 2 tsp vanilla extract
- ✓ 1 cup milk
- ✓ Assorted berries (strawberries, blueberries, raspberries) for decoration
- ✓ Edible flowers (optional) for added décor

Step-by-Step Preparation:

1. Preheat oven to 350°F (175°C). Grease and line three cake tins.
2. Melt the chocolate and butter in a bowl over simmering water. Once melted, stir in the sugar.
3. Beat in eggs, one at a time, ensuring each is well incorporated.
4. Sift in the flour and baking powder, mixing well.
5. Add vanilla extract and milk, providing a smooth batter form.
6. Pour into the prepared tins and bake for 40 minutes or until a toothpick comes out clean.
7. Allow cakes to cool. Once cooled, stack them, adding frosting between layers.
8. Decorate the top and sides with berries and optional edible flowers.

Nutritional Facts: (Per serving)

- ➤ Calories: 280
- ➤ Sugars: 24g
- ➤ Protein: 4g
- ➤ Fat: 15g
- ➤ Carbohydrates: 35g
- ➤ Sodium: 80mg
- ➤ Dietary Fiber: 2g

The "Tasty Chocolate Wedding Cake Decorated with Berries" is not just a dessert; it's a work of art. Perfect for momentous occasions, each slice carries the weight of cherished memories and the sweetness of future promises in Dessert Decadence style.

Recipe 95: Pecan Pie Brownie Bars Drizzled with Caramel Sauce

Dive into a world where pecan pie meets brownie! The "Pecan Pie Brownie Bars Drizzled with Caramel Sauce" offer a delightful fusion of flavors and textures, making them the epitome of Dessert Decadence. These bars are the ultimate treat for those who believe dessert is a sensory experience.

Servings: 16

Prepping Time: 25 minutes

Cook Time: 35 minutes

Difficulty: Intermediate

Ingredients:

- ✓ 200g dark chocolate, melted
- ✓ 150g unsalted butter, softened
- ✓ 200g granulated sugar
- ✓ 3 large eggs

- ✓ 100g all-purpose flour
- ✓ 1 tsp vanilla extract
- ✓ 200g pecans, chopped
- ✓ 100g light brown sugar
- ✓ 150ml heavy cream
- ✓ 2 tbsp caramel sauce

Step-by-Step Preparation:

1. Preheat oven to 350°F (175°C) and grease a square baking dish.
2. In a bowl, mix melted chocolate, butter, granulated sugar, 2 eggs, flour, and vanilla until smooth.
3. Pour the brownie mixture into the baking dish.
4. Combine pecans, brown sugar, 1 egg, and heavy cream in another bowl. Spread this over the brownie layer.
5. Bake for 35 minutes or until set.
6. Allow to cool, then cut into bars.
7. Drizzle caramel sauce over each bar before serving.

Nutritional Facts: (Per serving)

- ➢ Calories: 295
- ➢ Protein: 3g
- ➢ Carbohydrates: 32g
- ➢ Dietary Fiber: 2g
- ➢ Sugars: 25g
- ➢ Fat: 18g
- ➢ Sodium: 45mg

Relish the collision of classics in the "Pecan Pie Brownie Bars Drizzled with Caramel Sauce." These bars, dripping with sweet caramel, ensure that every bite celebrates rich flavors, marking a hallmark of Dessert Decadence. Perfect for any occasion, they're sure to be a hit!

Recipe 96: Blueberry Crumble with a Scoop of Vanilla Ice Cream

Indulge in a symphony of sweetness with "Blueberry Crumble with a Scoop of Vanilla Ice Cream." A burst of tart blueberries blanketed with a crispy topping, all married perfectly with creamy vanilla ice cream. It's Dessert Decadence at its finest.

Servings: 8

Prepping Time: 15 minutes

Cook Time: 45 minutes

Difficulty: Easy

Ingredients:

- 4 cups fresh blueberries
- 1 cup granulated sugar
- 1 cup all-purpose flour
- 1/2 cup rolled oats

- ✓ 1/2 cup unsalted butter, cold and cubed
- ✓ 1 tsp cinnamon
- ✓ 1/4 tsp salt
- ✓ 8 scoops vanilla ice cream

Step-by-Step Preparation:

1. Preheat oven to 375°F (190°C).
2. In a baking dish, mix blueberries with half the sugar.
3. Combine flour, oats, remaining sugar, cinnamon, and salt in a separate bowl. Add cubed butter and mix until crumbly.
4. Sprinkle the crumb mixture over the blueberries.
5. Bake for 45 minutes or until golden brown and bubbly.
6. Serve warm with a scoop of vanilla ice cream.

Nutritional Facts: (Per serving)

- ➤ Calories: 325
- ➤ Protein: 4g
- ➤ Carbohydrates: 55g
- ➤ Dietary Fiber: 3g
- ➤ Sugars: 38g
- ➤ Fat: 12g
- ➤ Sodium: 85mg

Every bite of "Blueberry Crumble with a Scoop of Vanilla Ice Cream" is a compelling dance of textures and flavors. A Dessert Decadence offering, this dish captures the essence of a comforting homemade dessert, making it a must-try for every sweet tooth.

Recipe 97: Dark Raw Chocolate with Hazelnut

Discover the rich intensity of "Dark Raw Chocolate with Hazelnut and Freeze-Dried Cherries." A Dessert Decadence masterpiece, this treat combines the profound allure of dark chocolate, the nutty crunch of hazelnuts, and the tart burst of cherries, ensuring every bite is an unforgettable experience.

Servings: 10

Prepping Time: 20 minutes

Cook Time: 3 hours (setting time)

Difficulty: Medium

Ingredients:

- ✓ 200g raw dark chocolate
- ✓ 100g whole hazelnuts, roasted
- ✓ 50g freeze-dried cherries
- ✓ 1 tbsp coconut oil & A pinch of sea salt

Step-by-Step Preparation:

1. Gently melt the raw dark chocolate and coconut oil in a heatproof bowl over simmering water.
2. Once melted, remove from heat and fold in the hazelnuts and freeze-dried cherries.
3. Spread the mixture onto a parchment-lined tray and sprinkle with sea salt.
4. Let set in the refrigerator for at least 3 hours or until solid.
5. Once set, break into rustic pieces and serve.

Nutritional Facts: (Per serving)

- Calories: 200
- Protein: 3g
- Carbohydrates: 15g
- Dietary Fiber: 2g
- Sugars: 10g
- Fat: 15g
- Sodium: 5mg

"Dark Raw Chocolate with Hazelnut and Freeze-Dried Cherries" is a luxurious journey for the palate. This Dessert Decadence dish offers a gourmet taste that fuses sweetness, tartness, and a hint of saltiness, making it a truly indulgent treat for those special moments.

Recipe 98: Strawberry Shortcake Ice Cream Bars with Cake Crumbles

Revisit your childhood with the creamy delight of "Strawberry Shortcake Ice Cream Bars with Cake Crumbles." A fusion of juicy strawberries and soft cake, these bars offer the perfect bite of summer sweetness.

Servings: 8 bars

Prepping Time: 20 minutes

Cook Time: 4 hours (freezing time)

Difficulty: Moderate

Ingredients:

- 1-pint strawberries, hulled and pureed
- 1 cup heavy cream
- ½ cup sugar & 1 tsp vanilla extract
- 2 cups vanilla cake crumbles
- 8 wooden popsicle sticks

Step-by-Step Preparation:

1. Mix strawberry puree, heavy cream, sugar, and vanilla extract in a bowl until well combined.
2. Pour the mixture into popsicle molds, filling them three-quarters of the way.
3. Sprinkle vanilla cake crumbles into each mold, pressing them slightly.
4. Insert popsicle sticks into each mold.
5. Freeze for at least 4 hours or until fully set.
6. Once frozen, remove from molds and enjoy!

Nutritional Facts: (Per serving)

- Calories: 250
- Total Fat: 14g
- Sugars: 25g
- Protein: 3g
- Vitamin C: 50%

These Strawberry Shortcake Ice Cream Bars capture the essence of a timeless dessert. The contrast between cold, creamy ice cream and the softness of cake crumbles is pure decadence. Dive into nostalgia with each bite!

Recipe 99: Delicious Freshly Baked Cinnamon Rolls

Indulge in the warm and comforting aroma of "Delicious Freshly Baked Cinnamon Rolls." With its soft, fluffy layers and sweet, spicy filling, this classic treat promises a bite of heaven every time.

Servings: 12 rolls

Prepping Time: 1 hour 30 minutes

Cook Time: 25 minutes

Difficulty: Intermediate

Ingredients:

- ✓ 4 cups all-purpose flour
- ✓ 1 cup warm milk
- ✓ 2 ¼ tsp active dry yeast
- ✓ ¼ cup granulated sugar
- ✓ 1 egg

- ✓ ¼ cup melted butter
- ✓ 1 tbsp ground cinnamon
- ✓ ½ cup brown sugar
- **For the glaze:**
  - 1 cup powdered sugar
  - 2 tbsp milk

Step-by-Step Preparation:

1. In a small bowl, dissolve yeast in warm milk and sit for 5 minutes.
2. Combine flour, sugar, egg, and melted butter in a large mixing bowl. Add yeast mixture and knead into a soft dough.
3. Allow the dough to rise for 1 hour.
4. Roll out the dough and spread a mix of brown sugar and cinnamon.
5. Roll the dough tightly and slice into 12 pieces.
6. Place in a greased baking dish and let rise for 20 minutes.
7. Bake at 375°F (190°C) for 25 minutes or until golden brown.
8. While still warm, drizzle with powdered sugar and milk glaze.

Nutritional Facts: (Per serving)

- ➤ Calories: 280
- ➤ Total Fat: 4g
- ➤ Sugars: 25g
- ➤ Protein: 5g
- ➤ Carbohydrates: 56g

Savor the symphony of sweet and spicy flavors in these cinnamon rolls. Perfect for breakfast or a dessert treat, their delightful texture and rich taste will leave you craving more. Embrace the sweetness!

Recipe 100: Matcha Green Tea Ice Cream

Indulge in the unique blend of earthy and sweet with "Matcha Green Tea Ice Cream." This creamy treat combines the antioxidant-rich matcha with velvety ice cream for a refreshing and sophisticated dessert experience.

Servings: 6

Prepping Time: 10 minutes

Cook Time: 30 minutes (Churning time)

Difficulty: Easy

Ingredients:

- 2 cups heavy cream
- 1 cup whole milk
- ¾ cup granulated sugar
- 2 tbsp high-quality matcha green tea powder
- 1 tsp vanilla extract
- Pinch of salt

Step-by-Step Preparation:

1. In a mixing bowl, whisk together sugar and matcha powder.
2. Add heavy cream, milk, vanilla extract, and a pinch of salt. Mix until well combined.
3. Pour the mixture into an ice cream maker and churn according to the manufacturer's instructions, typically 20-30 minutes.
4. Transfer to an airtight container and freeze for at least 2 hours or until firm.
5. Scoop and serve.

Nutritional Facts: (Per serving)

- Calories: 320
- Total Fat: 25g
- Sugars: 20g
- Protein: 3g
- Carbohydrates: 24g

Experience the harmonious blend of traditional matcha and creamy sweetness. Whether you're a tea lover or simply seeking a novel ice cream flavor, this dessert promises a delightful culinary journey to remember.

Conclusion

As you savor the final pages of this snack-centric masterpiece, one truth becomes apparent: snacking, often misconstrued as a guilty pleasure, can be both nutritious and gratifying.

"Delicious High-Protein Low-Calorie Snacks: 100 Inspiring Pictures" was meticulously crafted with you in mind. Oliver Brentwood has demystified the art of snacking, showcasing that indulging without compromising health is possible. Every recipe, bursting with protein yet mindful of calories, has been enhanced with an inspiring photo, making it easier to recreate these delightful snacks.

Reflect upon the versatile recipes you've uncovered, ranging from savory treats to sweet delights. Each one, tailored for those fleeting moments of hunger, ensures you're energized without the calorie overload. With this guide in hand, gone are the days of mindless munching; welcome the era of informed, delectable snacking that aligns with your wellness aspirations.

As snack times beckon in the days to come, revisit the pages of this book, drawing inspiration and experimenting with flavors. Share these innovative creations with loved ones, setting a new snacking standard. And remember, armed with suitable recipes, every snack can be an opportunity to nourish the body and please the palate.

Here's to guilt-free, scrumptious snacking, Oliver Brentwood

Printed in Great Britain
by Amazon